THE TRAGEDY OF STEALING

DR. D. K. OLUKOYA

THE Tragedy of STEALING

DR. D. K. OLUKOYA

The Tragedy of Stealing

© 2014 DR. D. K. OLUKOYA

ISBN: 978-978-920-110-5

Published July, 2014

Published by:
The Battle Cry Christian Ministries
322, Herbert Macaulay Street, Sabo, Yaba
P. O. Box 12272, Ikeja, Lagos.
www.battlecrystore.com
email: info@battlecrystore.com
   customercare@battlecrystore.com
   sales@battlecrystore.com
Phone: 0803-304-4239, 0816-122-9775

I salute my wonderful wife, Pastor Shade, for her invaluable support in the ministry.

I appreciate her unquantifiable support in the book ministry as the cover designer, art editor and art adviser.

All the Scriptures are from the King James Version

All rights reserved. Reproduction in whole or part without a written permission is prohibited. Printed in Nigeria.

CONTENTS

CHAPTER	PAGE
Though Hands Be Joined In Hands	4
The Tragedy Of Stealing	25
Stealing – The Foundation Of Poverty	48
Tenants In The Ground Floor	68
The Tragedy Of Lies	89
Five-fold Prescriptions For Overcoming Stealing	100

CHAPTER 1

Though Hands Be Joined in HANDS

DR. D. K. OLUKOYA

> *Though hand joins in hand the wicked shall not be unpunished But the seed of the righteous shall be delivered.* Proverbs 11:21

The scripture reveals that there are individuals who team up to do evil to others. The expression 'hand join hand' symbolizes co-operation, connivance, confederacy and conspiracy. In this case, the gang up or network is to cause harm and fulfill an evil agenda.

It means that no matter how tight the cooperation maybe, no matter how bright, intelligent or smart they may be, no matter how cleverly they conceal their evil plans, to protect themselves, no matter the wall they have built, no matter their techniques of hiding, no matter the kind of meetings they have held and no matter the agreement not to reveal their secret, the wicked shall not go unpunished. Whenever sin is in the driver's seat, you can be a hundred percent sure that shame is in the back seat. Wherever sin is present, Mr. Shame is usually there as well. The worst enemy that we have is our sinful heart, propelled and fueled by Mr. Flesh.

A couple had only one son and when he found that family poverty was too much to bear, he decided to go out to work in a foreign land in order to help his

THE TRAGEDY OF STEALING

parents. So the parents stayed in the village while the son went abroad. The son did not come back till after twenty years. By this time, he was prosperous and as he was returning home, he brought many gifts for his aged parents. Because he had left home for a long time, he could not remember their home address anymore. However, as he was passing through the village, somebody saw him and greeted him very well. The boy roamed around the street and tried to locate their house. Eventually, when he couldn't find it, he knocked on a door and a couple came out and welcomed him. He told them he was a traveler and that he came to look for something in this village and that he came to see his parents. Having been out for a long time, his parents couldn't recognize him anymore, he recognized them but he just wanted to pretend. They took him in, provided him hospitality, and told him that he could go and look for his parents in the morning. So he slept. He packed the gifts where he slept. At night, the couple started to plan. They said, "How else would God bless us more than this? This one is a total stranger, he has brought prosperity here. Let us kill him and take over all these things." They killed the man on the bed. The next morning a villager came and knocked their door. They came out and the villager said, "Congratulations, I saw your son yesterday." It then dawned on them that it was their son they killed.

SIN ATTRACTS CONSEQUENCES

When sin is on the driving seat of your life, shame is also always at the back seat. Sin hooks a man when he wants to obtain what he does not have at all cost. It is important for you to know that there is no small sin. When you come for a devotion service and begin to discuss in a way that disturbs others from flowing in the spirit, you are a sinner. There is no small sin.

The consequences of that small sin may be immeasurable. If you are stealing because you want to make some profit, let it be known to you that you shall not profit by sin. Anything you gain from sin would be returned with interest. Sin is like a small child playing with a snake. It may look very beautiful and interesting; but that is only so when the snake has not done its worst. I want you to know that every one of us has the power to choose our sin, but one thing we don't have is the power to choose the consequences of sin.

The way God has organized the world is that every sin has its punishment and consequences attached to it. So once you commit a sin, the punishment is automatic. And when sin enters, it would cause a cup of joy to leak. As soon as the seed of sin is sown, judgment is sure. Unfortunately, the Bible says one sinner destroys much good. The sin of one person can bring tragedy to many. For example, Jonah would have killed everybody in that ship because the Lord was not ready to negotiate with him at all. Perhaps as you are reading this book, you are the Jonah in your family. You are the reason why the evil wind is blowing on your family. If you are not doing the will of God, winds and storms will be blowing on you. Perhaps God has brought you to the Mountain of Fire and Miracles Ministries to do something and you refused to do it. If you refuse to do what God wants you to do, the wind and storms of life would be hard on your family.

The first time small pox struck India, it wrecked havoc to the populace and the recovery rate was slow. Even at that, the people who recover from small pox carry the mark till they die. You would always see the mark of the pox on the face of such people. There was a little boy that escaped from the ship and ran to India. He infected others and three million people died.

GOD JUDGES SIN IN HIS OWN WAY
The mistake we make is this, sin is not going to be judged the way you see it, it is going to be judged the way God sees it. And when God wants to start His judgments, where He would stop would be very strange to you.

A boy was tied and shot at the Bar Beach for stealing and when God wanted to start the judgment, He began with his mother who had a sugar daddy. From that to the one who was selling marijuana to him and to the one who was selling alcohol to him. From there to the madam who owned the bar where the boy drank pepper soup and the person who introduced him to robbery. So God would pack so many people together when He begins to judge sin. He won't judge it according to your opinion. What you and another person did, the repercussion of each may be completely different. If, for example, you are a sister and God called you to be a prophetess and He made a decree that through you shall be a seed that would save Africa and then you had an abortion, and that child you removed was the seed, your own repercussion of sin would be greater than the woman who had twenty abortions.

Prices of materials may rise and fall, but the wages of sin remains the same. The Bible says that the wages of sin is death. The most expensive thing in the world, beloved, is sin because for the purpose of sin God gave His own son to be killed. We have the academic sinners, the intellectual sinners, brain sinners, psychological sinners and so on. There are many new sinners everyday but there is no new sin, sin is still the same. What I want you to understand

THE TRAGEDY OF STEALING

is that wickedness never goes unpunished. You pay for the pleasures of sin with the coin of sorrow. And that sin you are covering up would eventually bring you down because sin is the greatest of all detectives. The Bible says, "Be sure, your sin will find you out."

A man strangulated a young girl after raping her. He killed the girl, dropped her on one bush path and went home. When he saw his wife, she saw that his coat was a bit rough and that he had lost one button. The wife asked him, "What happened to your button." The man couldn't tell his wife what happened, but he knew that surely the button must be at the site where he killed the girl. He couldn't rest again. Policemen arrived at the scene of the murder and looked for clues around. They found nothing, but one detective discovered the button and kept it in his pocket. He didn't tell anybody about the button. It wasn't in the newspaper that they found a button at the crime scene and everything went like that. But this man had no peace; something kept reminding him about the button, and he became so restless. Then one day, after few months, he went to that site, thinking he could find the button. Immediately he arrived there and was searching the place, the police arrested him. They said, "We know what you are looking for. You are looking for your button". His sin eventually found him out.

You that have children outside your normal marriage, your sin will find you out. That child will grow and eventually come back and destroy the family. Note this beloved, every sin, no matter how little, has a consequence. Even misusing your mouth has a consequence you need to understand this very well.

FORGIVENESS DOES NOT ELIMINATE DISCIPLINE

God is merciful and He forgives when we turn to Him in genuine repentance. He does not reject the cry for mercy from a contrite heart. The Scripture is replete with instances that when God forgives sin, He still disciplines the sinner. Let us examine some of these instances:

The first was when Miriam and Aaron spoke inadvertently against Moses, chiding and condemning because He married an Ethiopian woman. The Lord was angry because He had warned, "Touch not my anointed and do my prophet no harm."

Read the account of what happened:

THE TRAGEDY OF STEALING

And Miriam and Aaron spake against Moses because of the Ethiopian woman whom he had married, for he had married an Ethiopian woman.

And they said hath the Lord indeed spoken only by Moses? Hath he not spoken also by us?" And the Lord heard it.

And the anger of the Lord was kindled against them and He departed.

And the cloud departed from off the tabernacle and behold Miriam became leprous. White as snow and Aaron looked upon Miriam and behold, she was leprous.

And Aaron said unto Moses, alas my Lord, I beseech thee, lay not the sin upon us, wherein we have done foolishly, and where in we have sinned. Let her not be as one dead, of whom the flesh is half consumed when he cometh out of his mother's womb.

And Moses cried unto the Lord, saying heal her now O God I beseech thee.

> *And the Lord said unto Moses, if her father had but spit in her face, should she not be ashamed seven days? Let her be shut out from the camp seven days and after that let her be received in again".* Numbers 12:1

Note, beloved, that it was this Miriam that put Moses in the river. This was the same Miriam that called the attention of the daughter of Pharaoh to Moses. What was her sin? She spoke advertently against Moses. God's servant and anointed.

How was she disciplined? Numbers 12:15 says, "And Miriam was shut out from the camp seven days and the people journeyed not till Miriam was brought in again."

God disciplined Miriam until Moses cried, "Heal her now, O God!" God said, "I can forgive her, but forgiveness does not eliminate discipline." The Lord still dealt with her for seven days: She would have died but the Lord just had mercy.

Another instance in which God forgave sin but still disciplined the sinner was the case of David's sin of adultery with Bathsheba and the murder of Uriah. The Bible records:

THE TRAGEDY OF STEALING

And Nathan said to David, thou art the man, thus saith the Lord God of Israel, I anointed thee king over Israel, and I delivered thee out of the hand of Saul.

And I gave thee thy master's house and thy master's wife into thy bosom and gave thee the house of Israel and of Judah and if that had been too little, I would moreover have given unto thee such and such things.

Wherefore hast thou despised the commandment of the Lord, to do evil in his sight? Thou hast killed Uriah the Hittite with the sword, and hast taken his wife to be thy wife, and hast slain him with the sword of the children of Ammon.

Now therefore the sword shall never depart from thine house; because thou hast despised me, and hast taken the wife of Uriah the Hittite to be thy wife.

Thus saith the Lord behold I will raise up evil against thee out of thine own house and I will take thy wives before thine eyes and give them unto thy neighbour, and he shall lie with thy wives in the sight of this sun.

> *For thou didst it secretly but I will do this thing before all Israel and before the sun.*
>
> *And David said unto Nathan, I have sinned against the Lord, and Nathan said unto David, the Lord also hath put away thy sin thou shall not die.*
>
> *Howbeit, because by this deed thou hast given great occasion to the enemies of the Lord to blaspheme, the child also that is born unto thee shall surely die.*
>
> *And Nathan departed unto his house, and the Lord struck the child that Uriah's wife bare unto David and he was very sick.*
>
> *David therefore besought God for the child, and David fasted and went in and lay all night upon the earth.* II Samuel 12:7-16

What do you need to note here? God said, "I have forgiven." That forgiveness has removed condemnation; it has removed that sin from the record of God, but it does not eliminate the discipline. It does not remove the consequences.

THE TRAGEDY OF STEALING

A person who started a life of adultery after contacting HIV is now calling on God to forgive and heal him. God will say, "I have forgiven you, but you will still bear the consequence of your sin, though you will make heaven.

A man came to me some time ago and said his wife annoyed him, so he rose in his sitting room and said, "Father Lord, give me five minutes'

forgiveness because I want to panel beat this woman". So he asked God to forgive him and started beating his wife. One day he alighted from a bus at a Bus-Stop. All of a sudden, somebody shouted, "Thief, thief, this man removed my purse". Lagos people didn't hear him out. They pounced on him and beat him severely. Later they searched him and didn't find anything. But they had wounded him seriously and blinded one of his eyes. On his admission bed at the hospital, he started saying "O God, I am your child, why did this happen?" The Lord said, "Well, the consequence of beating your wife is what you have now." He said, "But I asked you to forgive me." The Lord said, "Yes, I have forgiven you but that does not eliminate the consequences."

Close your eyes, beloved, and pray this prayer. Anything that wants to destroy my destiny, blood of Jesus, clear it away, in the name of Jesus.

The other time there was a pastors' conference and an argument ensued at the conference. One pastor was so annoyed that he said, "Because of this thing you said to me, I will drop the Bible and deal with you." They left the conference. The vehicle they were travelling in had a serious accident. Everybody in that vehicle walked out without any scratch, but the pastor broke two legs. At Orthopedic Hospital, where they hung his legs, he asked "Lord what have I done?" The Lord said, "But you said you would drop the Bible?" He said, "But I asked you to forgive me." The Lord said, "Yes I did, if not, you would have died. Your Bible has been your support and your shield, and you said you were dropping it." He limbs today as a testimony for the discipline he had received.

There is no sin you can commit that God does not have the capacity to forgive you. God will forgive you, but you have attracted some consequences. There is nothing you can do about it. Those consequences will take their toll. You knew that something was bad, and unchristian, and you went along and did it. Bear it in mind that it would attract consequences. So right now, if you are deliberately planning to commit sin, in the book of Revelations the Lord said that after you read the whole of the Bible, you decide to continue to do evil, go ahead but "behold, I come quickly and my reward is with me."

THE TRAGEDY OF STEALING

Samson's hair grew again, but his eyes never got healed or opened again. Abraham got Ishmael, but the consequences are still with us now. God may forgive sin, but it will have consequences. Unfortunately, you will live with some of these consequences all your life. So every sin you are living in today is a foundation for your generation. The sins would find you and members of your generation out. That is why we have to be extremely careful. When Gehazi was going to collect the money from Naaman, had he known that it would affect his offspring, he would have said, "No, I don't want," but he went and planted evil seed in his generation.

AVOID GOD'S BLACK BOOK

In our secondary school in those days, there was a book in our school called Black Book. I used to remember our former principal telling us, "If your name enters the Black Book in this school, when I write your testimonial on leaving the school, it would be so hot, you will drop it." That was what he said. One day in a particular school, a boy used a knife on his friend and they reported to the principal. The principal wrote his name in the Black Book. The principal dried the knife with the blood and then put the knife inside the Black Book. He told the fellow, "You used knife on your friend; the name of that friend of yours is John. His blood is in your file" and we all laughed and forgot it.

Some years later, this fellow went to the United States of America to study and he was aspiring towards a very top position. The institution where he was studying wrote back to the school. The principal just wrote it there, John's blood is in his file." Just like that, every sin will find you out.

You think you are very clever, you can't be cleverer than sin; it would eventually find you out. There are some things you may do which may be corrected. For example, if you steal somebody's money and you return that money. There is no problem because the wrong has been corrected. But there are some sins you commit and there is no way you can correct them. So, forgiveness does not free you from accountability; you will pay for the consequences you acquired by your sin.

David committed the sin of sexual immorality, deception and murder. The consequences started very soon under the banner of sexual immorality. His own son raped his own daughter. His own son, Absalom, slept with his wife on the roof. David practised deception, very soon Solomon too did the same thing. Though David killed only Uriah, he lost three children: the baby, Amnon and Absalom. Sin had consequences. So if you don't want your children to become robbers, don't train them with stolen money. If you don't want your children to have broken homes, don't panel beat their mother before them. If you don't want your children to go into drugs, don't get involved in drug business yourself. If you don't want your daughter to be messed up, then don't mess up somebody else's daughter.

SIN DEMOTES AND KILLS

I was a teacher in the secondary school for some years and I was made a member of the disciplinary committee for teachers. A teacher was caught committing fornication with a student. They brought him to our disciplinary committee for the offence of immorality. The head of this committee was the vice principal. The man started to talk after they had found the teacher guilty. The man said, "Well, this thing that we are discussing here, we all do it. The only problem is that if they don't agree we don't force them." My temperature became high immediately. Then I stood up, brought out my Bible from my bag and opened Proverbs 11:21. I told him "You were made shepherd to these children. You have your own children too, now you are messing up other people's children. You who are supposed to be the head of this disciplinary committee and the vice principal. This is what you are saying. Know for sure that your sins would find you out." It was as though what I said was prophetic. One by one, I saw all those people later in life, the one that was not mad was sick.

Sometimes when people commit sin, they plead the blood of Jesus. The blood of Jesus does not eliminate the consequences of sin. It would only remove the condemnation. The only thing that can eliminate the consequences of sin is the mercy of God, nothing else. The trouble with the mercy of God is that the Bible says "I would have mercy on whom I would have mercy". That is, God's mercy is not guaranteed. Beloved, I want you to know that sin is success in nothing. Sin is self-inflicted nonsense. Sin invites death and death would vanish when sin disappears. Sin would obscure the soul. Sin can sometimes come as a friend, but the longer you stay in sin the less and less it bothers you. You become hardened, if you don't quickly run out of the sin. You know, if you take a frog and throw the frog into boiling water, the frog would jump out. But if you put the frog in cold water and you put the kettle on fire and begin to warm it little by little, the frog would not jump out until it is boiled to death. That is what sin does. The person would be enjoying the sin, eventually the sin would now turn on the person and would cause trouble. Only one leak in the ship is enough to sink the whole ship. One sin can destroy a person totally. Don't compare yourself with other people. Your life is different, your destiny is different. So don't say, "Well that person is doing it, I must do it." One little thing like this can cause great trouble.

THE TRAGEDY OF STEALING

Some years back somebody bought a new car and we were meant to deliver the car to someone in Ibadan. So we were inside the car and the driver that drove that day was the kind of driver who hated to see any vehicle before him. He overtook everybody and everything. The car was new, and we passed many vehicles. Anytime there was a car at the front, he would pursue and overtake the car. All of a sudden, it started to rain and the man switched on the wiper. The wiper did not function. The rain became heavier and he couldn't see the front again. He was forced to slow down and move to the slow lane. Then to our sadness, all the cars he overtook before were all just passing him. We had a new car but no wiper. So that small wiper sent us to the back. It is the same thing with sin. That small sin you don't think is serous is something that will send you to the tail of destiny.

CRY FOR MERCY

We need the mercy of God this day. We need to cry to Him for mercy. Mercy is obtained at the table of discipline. If you want to obtain mercy today, tell God the truth. All the evil friends that you are following about, there is a consequence. All the drinking and smoking have grave consequences. The satanic romance you are having with that brother or sister has its consequence. All those lies you are telling have their consequences. All the malice you keep and the grudge you bear also have consequences. "All the negative confessions and pronouncements you make have their consequences. All the rumour, the gossip, and the slander you engage in have consequences attached to them. All the misuse of your mouth and display of pride, there is a consequence for them. All the hypocritical act of coming to church and still taking alcohol has consequences attached to it. Your not using what God deposited in your life positively has a consequence. The man with one talent did not kill anybody. He did not use his talent. He buried it and because of that he went to hell fire. There is a consequence for you not running the agenda God has for your life. Are you stealing other people's money? There is a consequence.

You think you are paying somebody back in his own coin, there is a consequence for doing that. You are gossiping and backbiting, there is a consequence. It would be a sad thing if you appear at the gate of life and God's angel open the book of house fellowship, your name is there. They open the computer of MFM, your name is there. They open the book of baptism, your name is there. The Bible says one book shall be opened and other books too shall be opened and then another book shall be opened which is the book of life. They found your name in all those books but because of one stupid sin somewhere, they sent the person to hell fire. The person would have become Methuselah who came to the world and did nothing with his life. You should cry to the Lord now from your heart.

PRAYER POINTS

1. My Father, have mercy on me today, in the name of Jesus.

2. My Father, take me from the pit of bondage to the land of salvation, in the name of Jesus.

3. Anointing to live a holy and righteous life, fall upon my life, in the name of Jesus.

4. Thou power of God, withdraw my steps from the wrong way in the name of Jesus.

5. Holy Spirit, take my hands off my life and possess me.

6. Every rope of darkness tying me to shame and reproach, catch fire and burn to ashes.

7. Every power of bewitchment upon my spirit man die, in the name of Jesus.

► CHAPTER 2

THE Tragedy of Stealing

THE TRAGEDY OF STEALING

But the children of Israel committed a trespass in the accursed thing for Achan the son of Carmi, the son of Zabdi, the son of Zerah, of the tribe of Judah, took of the accursed thing, and the anger of the Lord was kindled against the children of Israel.

And Joshua sent men from Jericho to Ai which is beside Bethaven, on the east side of Bethel, and spake unto them saying, go up and view the country, and the men went up and viewed Ai.

And they returned to Joshua and said unto him, let not all the people go up. But let about two or three thousand men go up and smite Ai and make not all the people to labour thither, for they are but few. So there went up thither of the people about three thousand men and they fled before the men of Ai.

And the men of Ai smote of them about thirty and six men: for they chased them from before the gate even unto Shebarim and smote them in the going down wherefore the hearts of the people melted and became as water.

Vs 11, Israel hath sinned, and they have also transgressed my covenant which I commanded them: for they have even taken of the accursed thing, and have also stolen, and dissembled also. And they have put it even among their own stuff.

Therefore the children of Israel could not stand before their enemies, but turned their backs before their enemies, because they were accursed neither will I be with you anymore, except ye destroy the accursed from among you.   Joshua 7:1-12.

Shall not all these take up a parable against him, and a taunting proverb against him, and say, woe to him that increaseth that which is not his, how long? And to him that ladeth himself with thick clay. Habakkuk 2:6

What does it mean to steal? To steal means to take something without right, without permission, that which does not belong to you. Those things you took could be things, it could be money, it could be anything. It could be time. It could be somebody else's innocence. It could be somebody else's reputation. It could be somebody else's resources. It could be somebody else's property. It could be somebody else's wife or husband. But you took that thing without permission. The bible calls it stealing.

Stealing is to keep others from receiving what is rightfully theirs. When you withhold profit, withhold time, withhold recognition, withhold wages. You cheat or you defraud, that is stealing. It is not in vain that the Bible cries out loud and clear as part of the Ten Commandments, one of the Ten Commandments is, thou shalt not steal. That thou shall not steal is pregnant with meaning. There are so many things behind it. Stealing is

THE TRAGEDY OF STEALING

the most common crime in the society. If the majority of the members of a nation are thieves their leaders too would be thieves. Some people gave stealing various names but it is still the same thing. They say somebody is pilfering, is stealing small small quantities and insignificant items. There could be a bag of rice, you just took one spoon that even the owner does not know, it is still stealing. They call another method of stealing shoplifting. Somebody goes to a shop and begins to steal things from the shop while pretending to be a customer. Some people call it embezzlement, you take money that was entrusted to your care in a fraudulent way. Some people call it extortion, you obtain something wrongfully from another by threat, force, or abuse of authority. That is what is known as stealing. It is the commandment you may be paying little attention to because we are assuming we are not thieves. You may be likely committing theft but you may not even likely know that you are committing theft as far as the bible is concerned. And as believers we are unlikely to commit theft in the sense in which it is normally understood. This has very deep implications. Listen to me clearly to night.

God wants his children to prosper the right way. The bible says the blessing of the Lord maketh rich without adding any sorrow to it. If you obtain your prosperity in a way that is not godly, sorrow would be added to it. As far as bible is concerned, God wants us to have prosperity in the right way. You work for it, you do profitable investment and trading, you pray believing prayers. You could have godly inheritance. You could have godly gifts. Those are the ways God wants us to prosper. And like I tell you all the time I would tell you again loud and clear tonight. You can only become what God wants you to become, nothing more nothing less. If you want to become what God doesn't want you to become you become a monster. If you want to have what God does not want you to have He will take away what He has given to you. If you want to have what God has not given to you, you lose what He has given to you. Gehazi wanted to have what God did not give him and God gave him something to spend that money he has stolen. This is a very serious matter beloved. There are different categories of thieves.

There are those who take things that are not their own, they are thieves.
There are those who withhold belongings and supplies.
There are those who impose on another's generosity.
There are those who evade prompt payment of their debt.
There are those who violate personal honour.
There are those who extort things from others.

A brother entered a bus and in that bus was a sister at the back who did not care how much the brother had in his hand. So immediately the brother entered she said, brother we are here, you cannot be in the bus and people

THE TRAGEDY OF STEALING

like us are paying. So that man who did not budget for it or plan for it had to pay and it was the last money he had.

As he was paying again another sister said brother I am here too, it is not only her you will pay for. That is what the bible call's extortion. This is stealing. Those two sisters are thieves. When you are serving the God of materialism what you are after is clothes, cars, you are a thief. There is also a group of thieves we call robbers in the sanctuary. Stealing from the house of God is the worst offense anyone can commit. If you steal God's money what you are stealing is sawdust and nobody can eat sawdust and digest it.

There are those who steal by decision.

Unfortunately, there are some who steal because they inherited stealing. That is, the great grandfather was a thief, the grandfather was a thief, your father was a thief and now you are a thief.

There are unconscious thieves that is those who would arrive at the gate of paradise and they say sorry you cannot enter here because you are a robber and you say but I didn't steal anything and they bring out his tithe record and say you are stealing from God.

There are those who steal by force that is another category of robbers.

Beloved if you steal you break one of God's commandments Exodus 20:15, Which says thou shall not steal. If you are a Christian you are not to be a thief because Christ who lives in you is not a thief. If you steal you must make restitution beyond the initial value of what you took this is what the Bible is saying. If you cannot make restitution you should work for the one you have wronged until the debt is paid. If something you borrowed from somebody is damaged or stolen you should pay for it that is what the Bible is saying. If you find an item that does not belong to you, you should try to locate the owner or you should just leave it, to keep it is stealing. If you steal you break God's heart because you are breaking His law of love. These are very very serious matters. If as a believer you did not realize that stealing is a grievous sin then your conscience is asleep. If you declare that you cannot afford something and you cannot live without it then you are headed to hell fire. If you cannot afford it and you cannot live without it you should die rather than stealing because of the implications of stealing. Technical innocence may skillfully achieve in the court of law but you are still guilty before God. What you are saying to God is what you are giving me is not enough I must get something from somebody else. God hates stealing in all disguises with perfect hatred. The spirit of I saw, I coveted, I took, I hid has taken root in so many lives and this is a very serious tragedy.

THE TRAGEDY OF STEALING

WHY DO PEOPLE STEAL?

1. People steal because they want to be significant. They are craving for worldly success. They are rationalizing that they must have more than they have. They are envying what others have. They are desiring to outsmart others at another person's expense. This is the reason why most people steal

2. The second reason why people steal is because they are searching for security. They are afraid because they fail to trust God and they are unable to set themselves free from worry. Is a terrible situation but that is the truth.

3. Unbelief. A person who steals just does not believe that God can provide for Him. The person does not believe that God can prepare a table for him in the wilderness so he prepared his own table using his neighbours property. Beloved, stealing is self preparation of such evil table and such tables do not last. A person who trusts God with all his heart will never steal.

4. Covetousness. At least you are not satisfied with your own property where as Bible says godliness with contentment is a great gain, we brought

nothing to this world and it is certain that we are taking nothing out of the place. When you are secretly eyeing and envying somebody who has something you are yet to have, you are a thief. When you desire what belongs to another man by any means available you are a thief. When the children of Israel entered the Promised Land the first sin that was recorded against them was the sin of stealing. That covetousness graduated to stealing by Achan which put the whole nation into trouble. It is good to listen to this now if you are interested in going to heaven or you don't want your family to be put into trouble, and the Lord today is calling many people here into repentance.

WHAT IS STEALING ACCORDING TO THE WORD OF GOD?

Stealing is when you are jealous of other people and you are wishing that what they have might be yours. Stealing is admiring those who manage to cheat and get away with it. Stealing is when you are only scared by the consequences of being found out not that you don't desire to steal. The reason you are not stealing is because you are afraid that you would be caught and be jailed. So it is the fear that you have, if you are not going to be caught you will steal. There are many people who say I can't steal, you can only say that when you have access to money and you did not steal it you are still a thief inside.

THE TRAGEDY OF STEALING

When you wish that you could take something away from another person it is stealing according to the Bible. When you are a pastor you are ministering for gain then you are a thief. You are a spiritual armed robber. Look at all those pastors who are doing the work of God because of money they really never get the money. It is those who are interested in blessing people that are getting blessed.

Stealing is when you are ministering for a lust for others. Stealing is when you are teaching untrue doctrine because you want popularity. There are plenty of spiritual thieves around. They take away from people the means of salvation. They place trust and confidence not in the Lord but in themselves. When you do not agree that the good we do is the power granted to us by the Lord, it is stealing. Stealing is when there is anything in your life that is fascinated with the idea of getting something for nothing. This is why gambling too is stealing. You want to put ten thousand naira down and you want one million naira. Stealing is taking what does not belong to you. Stealing is using your company suppliers without permission, paper, biro, postage stamps, envelop, making phone call on the company which is private, is all stealing. All the clever confiscation. Somebody lent something to you and you keep it without returning it and you pretend that you don't have it you are a thief. You make the person to forget that he had lent it to you, it is stealing. Some even steal Christian books from people and keep it in their house and refuse to return it to the owner, you are a thief. If you use dishonest scale and dishonest cup to measure things for people you are a thief. All the putting the nice things on top and put the rotten ones below, you are a thief. All the cheating and the fraud is all stealing. When you make extravagant claims and promises you cannot keep, it is all stealing.

It is like that lawyer in Ghana, he was on the phone while they were installing his phone, but they had not completed the installation. So somebody was knocking on his door, he taught the person was a customer so he took the phone and said yes, that case from America we have won it, the one from United Kingdom we have won it too we are able to make twenty million cedis in that one. We have got one million pounds in the other one, of course we can handle your case. He said okay hold on I have a visitor now. So he placed his phone on his table and turned to the man who entered the office and said yes sir can I help you, do you need our services? The man said I am from the telephone company we have not connected this phone so what are you saying? Who are you talking to? He is not a lawyer but a thief.

When you withdraw something from someone when it is due to that person you are a thief. Somebody parks his car, you hit it and you dented the car and quietly reverse your car and ran away, you are a thief. When you begin to get possession of another person's property by means of using authority or force, you are a thief. All the kind of

THE TRAGEDY OF STEALING

charging excessive prices, excessive profiting is stealing. Kidnapping is stealing. Intentional negligence which results in loss to another person is stealing. You were employed as a security guard but you spend most of the time sleeping there because you know that if they come to see you nobody would ask you to refund, you are a thief. When you fail to return something to the faithful owner you are a thief. Failure to give to others what belongs to them, you are a thief. Arriving very late to work you are stealing. You leave early from work without permission you are a thief. You are converting company equipment into private business you are a thief. You are supposed to be working somewhere all you are doing is reading novels or reading magazines or you are even reading your bible in the place where you supposed to be working, you are a thief. When you are given one hour for lunch and you go away for four hours you are a thief. You are in your place of work and you hide in the toilet to read the Bible, you are a thief. All the cases of students cheating in class you are stealing. When you are claiming to yourself glory that is due to God you are a thief. All forms of counterfeiting or forgery is all stealing. Anybody working with a false certificate, you are laying a bad foundation for your destiny is stealing. They say small thieves steal from men but giant thieves steal from God. When you rob God glory due to Him you are stealing from God. When you are boasting about your spiritual achievement you are stealing from God. When you are boasting about how rich and how influential you are, you are stealing from God. Telling people about how intelligent you are when you did not manufacture your brain you are stealing from God. Refusal to give testimonies on what the Lord has done for you, you are stealing from God. Feeding unbelievers at birthday parties and telling them that God had spared your life you are stealing from God. When you ascribe the honour for what the Lord has done to yourself then you are stealing from God. The book of Malachi 3 says can a man steal from God? He answers the question and says yes. He says in which way have we stolen from you O Lord. He said through your tithe and offering. A good robber can steal from anyone. If you see somebody who steals from God, that person can steal from your hand bag if you stay by his or her side. This is a very common sin among believers. Many have completely forgotten about honouring the Lord with the first fruit of their increase. We did first fruit service recently, many people did not participate, they are stealing from God. The Bible says Honour the Lord with the first fruit of your substance so that your barn would be full. Some actually complain that the tithe is too much, they are stealing from God. You find some bookshops selling books that are not for sale, free books for evangelism they are selling it, they are all stealing from God. Are you stealing from God? If you are it is wiser to repent today. When you steal church money you are stealing from God. Perhaps, believers contribute money and gave it to you to keep then, you use it and fail to return it, you are a thief.

THE TRAGEDY OF STEALING

I could remember the time my wife was making clothes because she studied fashion and designing at a stage. There came a time when many sisters would make clothes, when my wife says, sister are you not going to pay? She would reply, Jesus paid it all. How can General Overseer's wife be fighting members to come and pay for clothes? It is stealing.

When God lays it in your heart to give a particular amount to his work and you cut it, it is stealing. A lot of people are stealing from God day by day. When you fail to tithe your time to God you are stealing from God, because that God you are stealing from can cancel the time you have. There are some people who would buy two thousand naira shoes but to buy ordinary Bible to improve their spiritual life, it is too expensive. There are those who steal from fellow man, they would bring out lying advertisements. Sometimes if you read our dailies you would be so surprised, you say how can they allow this type of advert. If you pay this money and bring this one you make your breast and buttocks larger, they are all lying. Even the so called Christians are patronizing them along with other people. You claim to be able to do a job but you cannot do it, you are a thief.

I remember when I was a scientist. I wanted to buy an equipment and we were interviewing the contractors and one lady came also. Her head gear was almost touching the roof of the room. We asked her question number one, what is the use of this machine you want to supply? She said I don't know I want to supply it, I must supply it do you understand me? If you want me to settle you, I would settle you don't ask me foolish questions. They are all stealing.

I want you to understand beloved when the Bible says thou shall not and it does not explain further, there are lots of things attached to thou shall not. It is the blessing of the Lord that maketh rich, it doesn't add sorrow to it. Most of what people call fast business today is clever stealing. Tenants stealing from their landlords when they damage their property and furniture. Those who are evading tax and telling lies. I have ten children, fathers and mothers, which is all a lie they are all thieves. All these bring down the wrath of God and hinder, multiple breakthroughs. Gambling is another form of stealing. A gambler wants to obtain money for which he has done no honest work and a gambler is practicing witchcraft. Two football teams decided to play and they have decided to win and you are asking them to hire you, you are a witch. Laziness at work is also stealing because you are paid to do the work. I have worked in many places, I have worked in various places in my life it is very difficult to see a company sacking a hard worker. A believer collecting sick leave when he is not sick is not only stealing but writing unprofitable invitation to sickness. When you are telling lies about an injury in order to collect compensation they are all stealing. We know a

THE TRAGEDY OF STEALING

woman who went and put POP on her leg to tell her company that she had broken her leg where as there was nothing wrong with that leg. But somebody in that company was not convinced and said how can you break your leg and you are smiling and look like this. They now asked a neutral doctor to check, the legs were okay, nothing was wrong when the doctor checked. She is a thief.

There was a brother who didn't want to go to where they wanted him to go on transfer, so he picked his foot with a needle in two places and he held his legs as if he was in pain and went back to work to say that a snake had bitten him. Listen beloved, the same measure you use to measure for your employers where you worked before would be used for you in your own company. So you better stop. I want you to understand this very well. There was a time in this country WAEC examination paper leaked. By the time they would trace it, it was somebody working inside the company who wanted to give the answer to his girl friend, the man did not steal the paper, he was just memorizing it line by line everyday so he was using his brain to steal. He is a thief in his head.

Lawyers steal when they take advantage of their clients. They use the ignorance of that client to make situations look very bad. Judges steal when they take bribe and pervert justice, doctors steal when they make a case look more serious in order to charge exorbitant fees. Doctors steal when they prescribe surgery on somebody who does not need it because they need the surgery to get more money. You are walking with somebody, drinking his own bottle of soft drink and you say where is my own, you are a thief.

Many of these things that people have done or are doing invite the curse of God and block prosperity. You know that his wristwatch was stolen and you are buying it, you are stealing and it is a serious matter. A thief can be armed with a gun, a thief can be armed with a pen they are all thieves. Many parents teach their children to steal by example, then they start beating the children latter. Your child that you say should sit in the shop knows that you bought an item for five naira but you are telling lies to the customer that it is forty naira so you have taught the child how to lie. There are people who celebrate yearly birthdays in order to raise money, they are thieves. Any church without any apology if you are distributing any envelope to unbelievers, that church is a thief. More than any other offense people who fill up the prisons are majorly thieves. The devil is a master thief. He stole a whole kingdom from Adam by deception and that is what is happening these days. It is possible too, apart from stealing from God, apart from stealing from fellow men, you can even steal from yourself. You decided to buy a cheap new testament Bible instead of a whole Bible, you are cheating yourself and stealing from yourself. You decided not to take time to pray, to read the word of God

THE TRAGEDY OF STEALING

you are stealing from yourself. Many young girls are stealing from themselves when they sell their virginity away cheaply. Fornication is stealing from yourself the virtue that God has given to you. Do you owe anybody now? Even those you can pay you are not paying? You are a thief. Did you pick or take money you did not remember who owns it? You need to add one fifth to it and return it to the Lord. Have you ever received a bribe? You must repent. Have you ever been using people's things secretly without their knowledge? You need to repent. Have you been feeding people with false information? You need to repent. Did your office send you somewhere and you went and stayed in your friends house and yet you got a receipt from the hotel that you stayed there, you are a thief, you need to repent. Are you working with false certificate then you are a thief, you should repent. Are you a lady, you are planning to marry a man inspite of the fact that you know that the man has a wife, then you are a thief. Did you promise a girl marriage then abandon her to run off to another person you are a thief. Are you a sister, have you stolen your marriage from yourself by being dirty, being aggressive, lazy, argumentative then you need to repent. There is serious danger when any form of stealing is in your life. You need to ask yourself serious questions whether there is any falsehood in your dealings. When you steal you give the enemy a chance to poison your breakthrough. When you steal you set up a chain of reactions that would affect your generation. When you steal the repercussion would return to you then expand later. When you steal you fire an arrow by yourself into your spiritual life. When you steal whatever you stole would have a voice and would be crying against the angel of your break through. When you steal you find the leprosy of Gehazi coming upon you and upon your generations. When you steal you could put the whole of your family even the nation into trouble. Whether you are stealing from yourself whether you are stealing from God, whether you are stealing from man when you steal you set up a chain of reactions that can turn your life upside down. There are many believers now who steal in the place of work, it is a disgrace and a shame. It is a shame when somebody commits fraud in the bank and he says he is a born again Christian. What kind of thing is that. If you are the type who would say, well I didn't steal too much, this one is small, nobody would notice it. If you fool people you can't fool God. If you say well, I don't really want to involve myself in stealing but necessity made me to do it. No the truth is you are a thief on the inside. Somebody says well everybody does it. Everybody doesn't do it, you did it. And the repercussion would follow. You could pray fire prayer for prosperity but if you are a thief you are getting the prosperity in one hand and putting it in a pocket with holes. Some people say well I stole and then I can give extra money to the Lord, the Lord does not want your stolen money the Lord is not interested in stolen money but in clean money. And I tell you it is not every offering that someone brings that God would accept. I want you to understand that very well.

THE TRAGEDY OF STEALING

Many years ago in 1994, we had this auditorium A, all other places were water logged and wooden pillars and all kinds of things, the system was very poor. And this auditorium A we bought for one hundred and twenty thousand naira in those days. A sister that God used to give us that money is still a member today. The whole of this place was swampy. People sometimes remove their shoes to get to church. It was at that level one man came to me for counselling, and he said man of God, I would give you two million naira so that you can build a beautiful auditorium in this place on one condition, if you pray for me to sleep. He said he hadn't slept for three months. If you pray for me and I can sleep you get two million naira. Immediately he finished talking the Holy Spirit said blood money. So I said sir, thank you very much I don't want your money, the two million naira you have and you cannot sleep you want to give it to me so that I will collect it then I would not be able to sleep. I don't want. He said you mean you are rejecting it? I said yes sir. I said but I would pray for you for a temporary suspended miracle so that you can see the power of God to give you enough time to go and repent and do away with your blood money. I want you to know this is a very serious matter. I want you to understand that when you take what you should not take you increase in sorrow. Many of us need to take a step tonight to catch the thief in our heart.

In Romans 13:10, Love worketh no ill to his neighbour therefore love is the fulfilling of the law.

1. So you must first of all understand God's standard concerning stealing. Understand that God is against it thoroughly. The thief cometh not but to kill to steal and to destroy.

2. You need to admit that your heart is deceitful and ask God to reveal to you your personal area of dishonesty. Knowing fully well that everything you do is seen by the eyes of God.

3. Make a commitment to total honesty no matter what the consequences may be.

4. You need to make restitution when you realize that you have defrauded someone which was what Zacheous said. Many need to make restitution. If how to make restitution is not clear write to us and tell us this is what I have done how do I restitute this kind of thing. You are a sister you claim to be born again but you have complementary cards of sinner men inside your bag you are a thief. And you need to throw away those kinds of things and make restitution. This is the true word of God and there is a reason God is telling us this today. The first time the voice

thundered mount Sinai. In Exodus 20:15, "Thou shall not steal". That voice made no exceptions, no conditions, no escape clauses, but thou shall not. It is God's word and God's law. And woe to the man, or woman, or boy or girl, who breaks the laws of God. And many things we take lightly the Bible does not take it lightly and the sad truth is that many people are guilty of one form of stealing or another. You are a pastor working under somebody, somebody gives you something you didn't tell your boss, it still stealing. God is here today with his mercy to forgive, provided you make your restitution. Have you been stealing your tithe? You need to repent tonight and ask God to forgive you.

PRAYER POINTS

1. My Father have mercy on me and change my life in the name of Jesus.

2. O God arise and destroy anything in my life that represents stealing in the name of Jesus.

3. Any power creating scarcity for me, your time is up die in the name of Jesus.

4. Axe of God, cut down every witchcraft tree of stealing battling my life in the name of Jesus.

5. Every cage of witchcraft fashioned to suppress my star, I smash you to piece in Jesus name.

6. Every power behind destructive habit in my life, die in the name of Jesus.

7. The Adam in me, come out and die by fire of God of Elijah in Jesus name.

CHAPTER 3

Stealing the Foundation of Poverty

> *For ye are not come unto the mount that might be touched, and that burned with five, nor unto blackness and darkness, and tempest, and the sound of a trumpet, and the voice of words; which voice they that heard intreated that the word should not be spoken to them any more (for they could not endure that which was commanded. And if so much as a beast touch the mountain, it shall be stoned, or thrust through with a dart: and so terrible was the sight, that Moses said: "I exceedingly fear and quake:)" But ye are come unto mount Zion, and unto the city of the living God, the heavenly Jerusalem, and to an innumerable company of angels.*
> Hebrews 12:18-22

Something terrible happened at Mount Sinai, when Moses went to God for the Ten Commandments. The Israelites were in trouble; it was a fearful experience, even Moses was afraid. God told him what the people should do and what they should not do and he wrote them down. Many people think they can go to heaven just by obeying the Ten

THE TRAGEDY OF STEALING

Commandments. The Bible says if you offend in one, you offend in all. The person who keeps all commandments and breaks one is the same as the person who breaks all.

In Exodus 20:15, God commands: "Thou shalt not steal."

These days, believers take many things for granted. They even pick some portion of God's words and say they are not important. They refer to some sins as not being too bad. The sad thing in the matter we are trying to bring up is the fact that, nearly all Christians are guilty of this way of life. A person who takes what does not belong to him, is stealing. The person who is overpaid and does not return it, or does not return the change from an errand, or takes money from his father's or mother's pocket, is a thief. If you do it to your spouse, it is stealing. Inflating prices, or deceiving people about the product you are selling, or you use false measurement, you are stealing. There is so much tragedy in the world today; even those who are meant to catch thieves are the ones that are stealing. It is one of the problems that we have in the world and it is likely to attract heavy judgment from God.

The government of a country decided to put the men in the Police Force to test, and to see if they were honest or not. The decision to pay their salary for that month by hand was taken. The pay packet contained an amount that was slightly higher than their normal salary. After paying ten people, only one came back to say that the money was more than what he should normally collect. This brought the conclusion that only 10% of the Police Force was honest. **It is unchristian to consider an overpayment as God's blessing.** Even possessing a lost but found object is not God's blessing, but stealing.

THE ROOT OF STEALING

1. **Unbelief** – A person who steals does not believe that God can provide for him or her; the person does not believe that God can prepare a table for him or her in the wilderness and so, he goes ahead to lay his own table with his neighbour's property. Such tables do not last as they are easily overturned.

2. **Covetousness** – Discontentment with what a person has; eyeing and envying other people to the extent of being ready to do anything to get what those people have.

THE TRAGEDY OF STEALING

One of the first problems that the Israelites had on their way to the Promised Land was the consequence of stealing. Achan stole a Babylonian garment from the spoil of their conquest and the whole nation was put in disarray. When he was found guilty, his entire family was stoned to death.

A whole family could suffer for the misdeed of a parent or ancestor. A woman who is fending for her children by prostitution is putting such children in trouble. A father who is stealing company property or money to take care of his children, is putting those children in serious trouble.

This message should send many people to the altar of repentance, including you reading it.
This world is not our home, we are just passing through. How can it be heard of that after preaching all over the place, your neighbours find you in hell? The neigbhours you kept disturbing with your noisy prayers and preaching.

FORMS OF STEALING:

1. **Stealing from God** – When you receive praises from people on what God has done, it is stealing. Glory and honour belong to God and when He does anything, we should

give Him all the glory. Boasting about spiritual exploits is ascribing to oneself, the glory and honour due unto Him. Boasting about your achievements, power and wealth, refusal to testify, is stealing. A believer that throws lavish parties and invites unbelievers to celebrate his or her birthday is stealing from God; it is God that kept that person alive till that day and not the friends.

> *Go to now, ye that say: "Today or tomorrow we will go into such a city, and continue there a year, and buy and sell, and get gain: whereas ye know not what shall be on the morrow. For what is your life? It is even a vapour that appeareth for a little time, and then vanisheth away. For that, ye ought to say: "If the Lord will, we shall live, and do this, or that". But now, ye rejoice in your boastings: all such rejoicing is evil. Therefore to him that knoweth to do go good, and doeth it not, to him it is sin.* James 4:13-15

2. **Non-payment of Tithe** – Malachi 3:8-10; "Will a man rob God? Yet ye have robbed me. But ye say: "Wherein have we robbed thee?" In tithes and offerings. Ye are cursed with a curse: for ye have robbed me, even this whole nation. Bring ye all the tithes into the storehouse, that there may be meat in mine house, and prove me now herewith, saith the Lord of hosts, if I will not open you the windows of heaven, and pour you out a blessing, that there shall not be room enough to receive it."

Those who do not pay their tithes are stealing from God and anyone who can steal from God can steal anything from anybody. That is why some people remain poor, although they earn good money. They are stealing from God and the Bible says it is a curse. Many people do not honour God with their first fruits. Some feel their tithe is too much for God and so they reduce it. All these people are stealing what belongs to God.

One day, I went to a bookshop and was browsing through a book which was imported from abroad, and there was an inscription on it saying: 'Free; not to be sold.' I was shocked because: that was supposed to be a Christian Bookshop. Are you stealing from God? You had better repent now! Are you a church worker and you are stealing from the offering bag or from the church purse? Even if you are a pastor and you spend church funds, you are a thief. Even if it is simple contribution made by children of God for a specific thing in the house of God and you spend it, and then start to dodge brethren so that they will not ask you, you are a thief and you have stolen from God.

If God lays a specific amount on your mind to give as offering and you reduce it, you have stolen from God. If you are buying fashionable things and you are begging a man of God for money to buy a Bible, you are a thief because; you could buy it with the money you spend on fashion. Some people **'borrow'** their tithe. Such things bring poverty. If you have been stealing from God in any way, you must repent now because the devil is very clever; he will encourage you to continue, so that you can end up in destruction.

3. **Stealing from fellow men** – If you sell fake or expired goods, you are stealing from those that are buying it. If you pose and get a job that you cannot do and you are being paid for it, you are stealing. Too much gain is extortion and it means stealing from fellow men. It is the blessings of God that make a person rich and does not add sorrow to it.

THE TRAGEDY OF STEALING

A man went to a herbalist for charms that would make him rich. The herbalist said he would get rich, but would die young. He said he did not mind. The herbalist said he would throw grains of corn on the ground for his cock and the number of grains it ate would determine the number of years that the man would spend on earth after becoming rich. He agreed. The cock ate two grains and refused to continue. The man tried to coax it, but it did not eat any more. The man became rich, but died two years later. The devil has no free gift; when he gives, he adds sorrow to it. Therefore, do not make any attempt to get help from the Devil. In fact, it is enmity with God.

A man was accused of what he did not do and he told the Judge that he should quake before God and do what is right. In the end, he got justice. Since that, he got the name 'Quaker.' The 'Quaker Oat' family was honest and truthful. They were farmers and would not sell any bad thing. People loved to buy from them and so, they became very prosperous.

Many years ago, if employers had vacancies, they would first consult pastors to recommend people they could employ. They knew that they could get honest and conscientious workers from the church. Today, the story is different. One has to be very careful with the people that call themselves Christians; they could be the ones to ruin the business, if care is not taken.

Many people do not like this kind of message, but we have to deliver it. Most 'fast' businesses are dubious; they amount to stealing. A tenant who refuses to pay his rent is stealing from the Landlord. Gambling is stealing. Laziness in the place of work; tax evasion, going on sick leave without being sick, are all forms of stealing. The same measure that you use for people will be used for you when you too have your own company. Many people steal things belonging to the company and claim that others are doing it. As a child of God, if others are doing anything that is sinful, you should stand out and not do it. You should be a model wherever you are.

Examination malpractice is stealing. Lawyers who take advantage of client's ignorance to shift blames on them are thieves. Judges who pervert justice are thieves. Doctors who tell patients that their cases are serious, and need a lot of money for treatment are thieves. Children who take advantage of their parent's illiteracy to get money for school materials and not buy them, are stealing from them. Such children could fail their examinations because of that. When you trickishly get something from someone, you are a thief. If you force people to pay your bus-fare, or pretend not to have and so, make them buy things for you, you are a thief. Actions like these block prosperity. If you force people to reduce the price of their goods, you are stealing from them.

> **Know ye not that the unrighteous shall not inherit the kingdom of God? Be not deceived: neither fornicators, nor idolaters, nor adulterers, nor effeminate, nor abusers of themselves with mankind, nor thieves, nor covetous, nor drunkards, nor revilers, nor extortionists, shall inherit the kingdom of God.**
> I Corinthians 6:9-10

The person that steals with the aid of a gun and the one that steals by changing amount with his pen are the same. Many people teach their children to tell lies and steal, by doing it, very soon the children will follow in that path. Some parents use their children to get money from other people by telling lies about their situations.

Someone came to ask me for some money for a fast business and I was sure that there was something dubious about it. I told him that he should not go into it; that it was better for him to die the death of a righteous man than to die with filthy riches. I prayed with him in a way such that the lord would open his eyes to the fact that, he should not go into that business. He told me that he knew I would not give him the money; that he had been warned not to come to me for it. He left in anger and I did not see him until about a year later. Apparently, he got the money from somewhere and went ahead, but he was apprehended by the police and was in jail for some months. He was too ashamed to tell me that he should have listened to me.

More than any other offence, stealing puts many people in prison. It ruins governments and nations. Unfortunately, even the people that call themselves children of God and pastors, use dubious means to get money from people. Many pastors do not talk frankly to people; so that they will not stop coming to their church and so that the offering will not decrease. Therefore, they will stop saying the truth that will change people's lives.

As a man of God wanted to start preaching, the Lord laid in his heart that he should not preach on the topic that he had prepared, but that he should preach on Isaiah 35:8, which says; **"And an highway shall be there, and a way, and it shall be called 'the way of holiness; the unclean shall** not pass over it; but it shall be for those: the wayfaring men, though fools, shall not err therein." He obeyed God and after the sermon, the church committee warned him not to preach that kind of message again. The following week, the Lord told him that he should still preach on that verse and he did. They warned him again and he said he had heard. The third week when he got to the church, the seats were empty and the committee scolded him that he had sent the entire congregation away. His allowances were withdrawn, but he continued to do what God asked him to do. He suffered for a while, but suddenly, God arose and provided for him mightily.

> *Confirming the souls of the disciples, and exhorting them to continue in the faith, and that we must through much tribulation enter into the kingdom of God."*
> Acts 14:22

4. **Stealing from oneself** – When you do not pray or read the Bible and spend time in the presence of God, you are stealing from yourself. When you dodge fasting and prayer meetings or you do not obey the Holy Spirit when He says you should do one thing or the other, you are stealing from yourself.

One day, a woman came to report her husband to me, saying all sorts of things about him. As I was about to pray with her, the Lord ministered to me that she was an adulterer. I stopped praying and asked her why she was going about with other men. She could not deny it and said she was doing it because they were poor. I told her that it was sinful and that she was stealing from herself. I told her that she should be ashamed of herself for selling her body for chicken feed. **Many girls sell their virginity for a plate of rice or ice cream.** Some young men take advantage of naïve girls and have sexual intercourse with them. Sometimes, some of these men find out that they have been infected or are haunted spiritually.

A young man thought he had had a nice time with a girl and by the following day, he started to see the girl in every corner in his office and at home. They thought he was hallucinating and took him to spiritualists. He continued to see the girl and she would even laugh at him. Eventually, he was taken to a Bible Believing Church, where he was led to Christ and he got born again. He realized the gravity of living a sinful life. The Lord touched him and he was healed.

THE TRAGEDY OF STEALING

> *Come now, and let us reason together, saith the Lord: though your sins be as scarlet, they shall be as white as snow; though they be red like crimson, they shall be as wool.* Isaiah 1:18

God is ready to cleanse anyone who is ready for cleansing. The accumulation of things that do not belong to you will bring trouble. Do you owe someone and you are not ready to pay back? You had better repent now and come back to the Lord. Do you steal from God? Do you pick people's objects that got missing? Do you receive bribe? Do you use people's telephones or cars without telling them and you rub off all the traces that will show that you've used such things? Do you evade tax? It is stealing and you must repent. Are you planning to become the wife of a married man? Are you thinking of jilting your fiancée because you have found another lady who is rich? All these things, hinder the favour of God and make His face not to shine on people. Are you stealing from your marriage by being hot-tempered, aggressive, argumentative and dirty? This applies mostly to ladies; once they are married, they take things for granted, they steal from their marriage and in the end could lose the happiness in being married.

Today, I would like you to do what Zacheus did, he made up his mind to return all that he took from people through dubious means. Jesus told him that salvation had come to his house on that day. If you are the type that cannot do without thinking evil, you are stealing from yourself. If you can not do away with sinful and harmful habits like drinking, alcohol, smoking, illicit and premarital sex, lying, worldly fashion, seductive wears, pornography, etc, you are stealing from yourself.

The son of a renowned Nigerian artiste gave his life to Christ and said he felt sorry for anyone who had ever sat down to watch his father's plays or films. This is because those plays and films were produced with the aid and use of occultic powers, which diffused some unseen things into the lives of the people watching them. I also feel sorry for Christians who spend hours on end, watching films. They are stealing from themselves. Pride, cheating, falsehood of any kind, is stealing. Today, I would like you to be honest with yourself. The time has come to totally relinquish anything that the enemy has in your hands. Anything that you acquired through falsehood, anything that is not of God, you must do away with them, right away.

THE TRAGEDY OF STEALING

And the Lord spake unto Moses, saying: "If a soul sin, and commit a trespass against the Lord, and lie unto his neighbour in that which was delivered him to keep, or in fellowship, or in a thing taken away by violence, or hath deceived his neighbour; or have found that which was lost, and lieth concerning it, and sweareth falsely; in any of all these that a man doeth, sinning therein. Then it shall be, because he hath sinned, and is guilty, that he shall restore that which he took violently away, or the thing which he hath deceitfully gotten, or that which was delivered him to keep, or the lost thing, which he found. Or all that about which he hath sworn falsely; he shall even restore it in the principal, and shall add the fifth part more thereto, and give it unto him to whom it appertaineth, in the day of his trespass offering. And he shall bring his trespass offering unto the Lord, a ram without blemish out of the flock, with thy estimation, for a trespass offering,

> *unto the priest. And the priest shall make an atonement for him before the Lord: and it shall be forgiven him for anything of all that he hath done in trespassing therein.*
> Leviticus 6:1-7

If after reading this message you find yourself guilty, you have to make restitution; so that such things will not cause a hindrance to your relationship with God. If a drunkard falls and dies and goes to hell, the person who sold the drink to him too will share in the judgment for the loss of his life, so also will the producer. The Bible says: **"Though hand join in hand, the wicked shall not be unpunished: but the seed of the righteous shall be delivered."** (Proverbs 11:21)

Today, you have to be frank with yourself. Examine your ways and see if you are doing what God expects of you. If you have been stealing from God, or people, or yourself, it is time to make restitution and come back to the Lord. Do not deceive yourself.

The things we have discussed in this book, form the foundation of poverty in the lives of some people. If you have stolen from someone who is under God's curse, you have shared in that curse. Ask the Lord to forgive you. Ask Him to restore to you, all that you lost through stealing. God is the Alpha and Omega; He can do all things. He can reverse anything. How can it be heard that after going to church and carrying your Bible all over the place, you end up in hell. Talk to the Lord sincerely. The baby you aborted would have grown up to be somebody, therefore, ask the Lord to forgive you and silence the blood that is crying against you.

TAKE THESE PRAYERS WITH AGGRESSION AND DETERMINATION:

1. I make a covenant with my eyes this day, you shall not send me to hell fire, in the name of Jesus.

2. I make a covenant with my flesh this day, you shall not send me to hell fire, in the name of Jesus.

3. Fire of God, quench every inordinate thirst in my soul, in the name of Jesus.

4. Every dragnet of hell fire, break to pieces, in the name of Jesus.

5. Power to discipline myself, fall upon my life, in the name of Jesus.

6. O Lord, give me a mind like that of Christ, in the name of Jesus.

7. Anything in my life, opening the door to the enemy, die, in the name of Jesus.

8. All my enemies, hear the word of the Lord, you must surrender in shame, in the name of Jesus.

9. Every power from the graveyard working against my breakthroughs, scatter, in the name of Jesus.

10. Any evil tree planted against me, dry up, in the name of Jesus.

11. Every agent of nakedness and poverty in my life, fall down and die, in the name of Jesus.

12. Arrow of shame fired into my life, backfire, in the name of Jesus.

13. Every power sitting on my breakthroughs, die, in the name of Jesus.

14. Altar of failure assigned against my life, scatter, in the name of Jesus.

15. Every breakthroughs that stealing has stolen from my life be restored back by fire.

▶ CHAPTER 4

Tenants in the Ground Floor

DR. D. K. OLUKOYA

Buy the truth and sell it not, also wisdom and instruction and understanding. Proverbs 23:23

I want to make some important statements about truth now.

1. You will lose every battle you fight against the truth. Once it is the truth, there is no way you can win.

2. The truth is very stubborn and indestructible. The truth can never die. If you like attach an explosive to the truth and ignite it and allow it to explode, it will not die. Slam it on the floor, it will not die. Use your hammer on it, it will not be sufficient to kill it.

3. Where truth is present, God is there. The reverse too is true, where lies are present. Lucifer would be there because the Bible says he is a liar and the father of lies.

4. Lying is always afraid of examination but truth invites examination.

5. The truth shall always prevail no matter what you do about it.

THE TRAGEDY OF STEALING

6. No matter what you believe, it doesn't change the truth. If we say "This is the sun", and you say "I don't believe this is the sun", it doesn't change the truth. "I am a professor of that" it doesn't change the truth. After all you are a professor because there is no Goliath. When Goliath comes we would know who professors are.

7. If you ignore the truth, it will not kill it. That is why they say no matter how fast lies travels, the truth would always catch it up.

   Beloved, no matter the argument you engage in, the truth is always the strongest argument. So when Pilate asked that question in the Bible, "What is truth?" He was asking a very deep question.

8. Anytime the truth is blocking your way, be sure you are headed towards the wrong direction.

Four students went to play so they did not come to school, part of the reasons they didn't come to school that day was because there was going to be a test. So they ran somewhere so that they would not participate. The next day, they came to school and they told the teacher that when they were coming the previous day, the car bringing them had a flat tyre and that the extra tyre too was bad. That was why they could not come. So the teacher said, "Okay, but are you aware that we had a test yesterday?" They said, "Yes". The teacher added, 'You will do your own now." He now took those four students and put them in the four corners of the classroom, there was no way they could communicate. The teacher gave them a sheet of paper each and said, "I am only going to ask you one question. Which tyre got punctured? Is it the front one, the back one, the one on the left or on the right? So start writing". It wasn't long when one of them said, "Sorry sir, no tyre was punctured". No matter how far lies travel, truth would catch up with it.

Jesus stood before Pilate and told him, "I came to testify to the truth." The man asked, "What is truth?? If you read your Bible well, there are ten great truths in the Bible.

1. In Isaiah 65:16, the Bible says "That he who blesseth himself in the earth shall bless himself in the God of truth and he that sweareth in the earth shall swear by the God of truth, because the former trouble are forgotten and because they are hid from

mine eyes." God is truth and the ultimate reality. So, the first truth is God.

2. In John 14:6, the Bible says, "Jesus saith unto him I am the way the truth and the life. no man cometh unto the father but by Me." So the second truth is Christ.

3. In 1 John 5:6 reads, "This is He that came by water and blood, even Jesus Christ not by water only but by water and blood. And it is the Spirit that beareth witness because the spirit is truth." So the third truth is the Spirit of God.

4. Daniel 10:21 reads, "But I will shew thee that which is noted in the scripture of truth and there is none that holdeth with me in these things, but Michael your prince." The fourth truth is the scriptures.

5. In John 17:17, the Bible says, "Sanctify them through thy truth, thy word is truth." The fifth truth is God's word.

6. Gal. 2:5 reads, "To whom we gave place by subjection, no, not for an hour, that the truth of the gospel might continue with you." The sixth truth is the gospel.

7. Psalm 119:142 the Bible says, "Thy righteousness is everlasting righteousness and thy law is the truth." The seventh truth is the law of God.

8. Psalm 119:151 reads, "Thou art near O Lord and all thy commandment are truth." The eighth truth is God's commandment.

9. Micah 7:20 says, "Thou wilt perform the truth to Jacob and the mercy to Abraham which thou hast sworn unto our fathers from the days of old." The nineth truth is God's covenant.

10. 1 Timothy 3:15 the Bible says, "But if I tarry long, that thou mayest know how thou oughtest to behave thyself in the house of God, which is the church of the living God, the pillar and ground of the truth." The tenth truth is the house of God.

CLING TO THE TRUTH ALWAYS

Beloved, take note of this very well: truth is truth, even if everyone is against it. Lie is lie even if everybody is supporting it. I counsel you today, beloved, be ready at all cost to hold fast to the truth.

THE TRAGEDY OF STEALING

Prefer to lose your position, your possession or money than to tell a lie. Like Meshach, Shedrach and Abednego, be willing to go through the fiery furnace of fire than to worship the image of Nebuchadnezzar. I counsel you, beloveth, run the risk of being poor instead of agreeing with a lie. It is better for you not to have money in your pocket than to have money of lies in your pocket.

In the early seventies, a woman went to deliver her baby in the hospital and she couldn't afford to pay the doctor, which was around two hundred naira. The doctor, because of his past experience with patients not paying him, decided to lock up the woman and the baby until she paid. One day, the woman realized that the naming ceremony was getting close and the doctor had refused to release them because she could not pay. She now devised a technique to bring the baby out of the hospital. She got a black polythene bag, put the baby inside the polythene bag, put rubbish on top of the baby and said, "Matron, open the door. I want to go and throw this thing into the dust bin." The matron thought it was just rubbish she wanted to throw away. That was how she escaped with her baby without paying. That baby has become an adult and he is heavily in debt. Why? The foundation of his life was built on a lie, and that foundation is now following him about.

Close your eyes and pray like this: Every falsehood in my foundation that is now troubling my destiny, blood of Jesus wipe them away, in the name of Jesus.

There are so many people all over the world. They copy our prayer points, and messages. They use them and things happen. There are so many who come to learn a few things from here and they would go out and become commercial prophets. But the truth is this, if it is not panadol, it is not panadol, no matter what name you call it.

I had a sister in my counselling room some time ago. She said, "General Overseer, I want to ask you a question. Don't be annoyed, you just tell me the truth." I said, "Yes, what is the question?" She said, "General Overseer, is it true that there was a particular pastor that left this church and that pastor is the founder of Mountain of Fire. Then, one way or the other, they threw the pastor out and you took over." My first reaction was to laugh until my tummy was paining me. Fortunately, I am a person who keeps records. So, I went into the list of all the students I have trained. I found the name of the pastor on the list of the first students I trained. I went into the results of the examination that I conducted for them. I found out that out of the twenty two students, this man was number twenty. When the sister saw this piece of information, she said, "God forgive me. How can somebody who was in twentieth position claim that kind of thing?" The sister told me that some people actually believe that man. But the bottom line is this, if it is not panadol, it cannot be panadol. You can call it all kinds of names. A person can stand up one day and say, "I am the greatest Elijah." Infact, he can claim Apostle Elijah as his name and say he is the grandfather of Elijah in the bible. No problem, very soon the prophets of Baal would come and say, "Apostle Elijah, bring down fire." When he cannot bring down the fire, the moment of truth has arrived. Everybody will know that this one is not Elijah. Beloved, anybody who can sit down and decide to tell lies is already rotten inside.

Many years ago, I was invited to the University of Lagos, Nigeria by the student union and my topic was "How to Pass Examinations without Cheating". When I got there, I greeted them very well and requested that they allow me to change the topic to "How to Cheat in Examination without Passing". So I told them, 'You want to cheat? Keep cheating. Cheat very well, but it will backfire." I then told them what would happen if they cheat and it backfires.

Truth is like oil, it would always rise to the surface. Truth is the shortest distance between two points. The Bible nailed the coffin in the head completely when it said, "The time is now, they that worship God must worship Him in spirit and in truth." So without truth, you can't worship God.

THE ANATOMY OF LIES

When truth begins to decay in a life, that is what we call a lie. The Bible describes lies as the identity and stock in trade of the wicked.

> ***The wicked are estranged from the womb, they go astray as soon as they be born speaking lies.***
> Psalm 58:3

You need to understand what constitutes a lie. A lie is a deliberate untrue statement with the intention to deceive. Many believers are living their lives on a lie, many are believing lies. There is no foundation built on lies that can stand. There is something they call "white lie". That is an untrue statement, but it appears harmless and unimportant. The person is even feeling justified that he is telling the lie. That was what Annanias and Saphira did. They sold the land. Nobody asked them to sell it or to bring the money. When they brought the money, Peter asked them, "Is this how much you sold it for?" They said, "Yes. That was white lie. What happened to them? They fell down and died?

There is something some people call half truth, something partially true, but is not completely true. It is still a lie. There is something the legal practitioners call perjury. You give a false testimony. After you have sworn that you would not tell lies, they fire the first question at you and load of lies came out. When somebody says I have decided to follow Jesus, and you are a worshipper of idols, then you are telling lies, you are in trouble. There is something called deception. That was, you intentionally give a false impression. You are giving two different parties two different impressions. Your actions are contrary to what is being said. It is very disheartening.

There is a type of lying called pathological lying. This is when lying has become second nature or part and parcel of a person. We also have compulsive lying, purposeless lying and lying without feeling guilt. When you can't find the truth in the house of God then the statement of the scripture again comes to mind. That judgment shall start in the house of God. So you can tell lies through deceptions, omission and vain flattery. That is, you are praising the person, whereas it is a lie. You can tell lies through slander. And note this beloved, you can tell a lie through keeping quiet. You can tell lies through half truth. You can tell lies through double dealing. If you see group B, you tell them one thing, if you see group A you tell them another thing. Then two people begin to fight because you have ministered destruction to the two parties. It is very terrible. No man has a memory good enough to be a successful liar. One way or the other, one day your memory will fail you.

Lies must always be clothed but truth is always naked. A lie is always a crippled person because it would need a second lie to survive. When you are telling half the truth, then you are telling a whole lie. Before you deceive other people, the first person you are going to deceive is yourself. If you begin to add certain things to the truth, then you are subtracting from that truth and it will become a lie. Somebody said a lie can travel out half way round the world while the truth is still putting on its shoes; by the time the shoes are on, it catches up in one second. Beloved, if you are a true child of God that is filled with the Holy Spirit and the truth is inside you, you will find it very difficult to tell lies. You will sweat and find it difficult in telling one, but if the spirit of truth is not in you, lies will flow easily. The anointing of lies just comes and the person would just talk. Husbands tell their wives lie. Wives too tell

THE TRAGEDY OF STEALING

their husband lies. Lies plus lies is equal to the lies. And they now have children who have come to understand daddy as a manipulator and a liar. They know that mummy too is very clever at it.

When we were in school several years back, we had a terrible teacher who, anytime they wanted to shoot an armed robbers at Bar beach in Lagos Nigeria, he would take us there and say, "Come and see the end of a small thief that became big." Something happened one day, an armed robber was about to be shot when he requested to speak with his mother. They brought the mother close. By the time the mother moved close, he used his teeth to grip her ear. It took the efforts of the soldiers to take the woman away and he said, 'when I was stealing biro in school you didn't stop me, when I was stealing money you were sharing it with me, that is why I am here now".

Truth is always in existence but falsehood has to be invented. A lie would always stand on one leg, but the truth would stand on two. Lying is a child of fear in one form or the other. One thing I have noticed is that I am yet to see a liar that has prospered at any age. Lying is like drunkenness. When people feel that the truth is very dangerous, they begin to tell lies. Instead of saying, "Sorry I have other plans. I won't be able to come to this program," he said "I am too tired to come", that is a lie. Somebody is really angry and instead of saying, "This thing you are saying, this thing you are saying, I am very angry." He would say "Well, anything you want is okay with me". Instead of saying "I am feeling very sad." He would say, "I have headache. Don't talk to me now." Instead of somebody to say, "Excuse me, my sister. I am no longer interested in this relationship. I don't want to marry you again." Instead of telling the person "The book you gave to me, I don't even know where it is." He would say "I have started reading it. I have almost finished the book." You do not even know where you kept it. All this little small things are what the Bible calls little foxes that spoil the vine".

One man told his wife, "I have a contract in a big city. I am going there". The man went to his strange woman somewhere in another city. He didn't know that someone had placed magun on the woman. Magun – thunder bolt which literally means don't climb. The wife later got a phone call and the caller told her that her husband was dead. The woman asked, "where." The caller mentioned the name of the city. She said "No, my husband left this morning. I drove him to the airport. She didn't know that immediately she dropped the man, he took a taxi to the garage and boarded a vehicle. A liar is treading on very dangerous grounds.

THE TRAGEDY OF STEALING

The job of a pastor is something that is tough. Sometimes you post a young pastor to a place and very soon they would write a letter that this one doesn't have the experience. Sometimes, when you post people with gray hair to them, they run back to the General Overseer and say, "This one is too old. He is not dynamic; we want a young person." Sometimes if the wife of the pastor is very strict who takes no nonsense, but the pastor is very soft, they would say the wife is a witch. If the man is preaching and he spends too much time, they would say "he wastes their time". When the sermons are too short, they say, "Is this what would get us to heaven?" If the man is telling them the truth, they would say he is very offensive. If he is not telling them the truth, they would say he is a hypocrite. Such is the nature of minister's job. So people in our position have to be very careful. We have to intercede regularly for whoever is a pastor.

I was in an aircraft sometime ago. Normally, the General Overseer receives about two hundred letters per day. So, I carried all my letters inside the plane and was reading them. There was a white woman by my side who was looking at me carefully. She didn't talk to me, but she was watching. When she couldn't hide it and the plane was about to land, the woman said, "Excuse me sir, what is your profession?" In my life I have never seen such a pile of letters, especially handwritten letters". I said, "I am a pastor. She said 'really', so these letters are letters of problems? I said 'yes'. She now asked why did you choose such a difficult profession?' I now confused her more I said, "Necessity is laid upon me." She didn't understand that one at all. The plane landed and I didn't talk to her again. So the job of a pastor is a very tough one. Many of you pray here and you go home, sometimes by the time the pastor arrives in his bedroom, one demon would be waiting there and say, "Excuse me, who asked you to pray for that person?"

THE ROOTS OF LYING

The root of lying is present because there is a sin nature in us. It is because we have a tendency not to trust God who cannot lie. We have a tendency to listen to the devil who is the father of lie. Unfortunately, we have a desire to sometimes deceive ourselves to hide the truth.

1. The first root of lying is our Adamic nature: our fallen nature.
2. The second root of lying is fear. You were afraid of being discovered and you told lies.
3. Envy. A desire for personal profit or jealousy towards others. This is mother root of lying.

4. Self promotion. You want to look good before others. You want to receive praise and recognition.
5. Self protection. You want to escape some negative consequences.

WHAT IS THE SOLUTION?
1. You have to repent from all lies that you have ever told.
2. You have to establish a nature of accountability.
3. Meditate on scriptures.
4. Consciously tell the truth.
5. Know the dangers of living your life with lies. God hates liars. Liars bring negative consequences. Lying would compound your problem with God. Lying to others is lying to God. Lying would be exposed with time. Lying would not go unpunished.
6. Know that telling the truth is tough, and you cannot please everyone. You can speak the truth in a loving way. Know that you are not a perfect person, so don't tell lies.

Gift Smith, a very powerful man of God, was having a crusade. He was preaching what we would call the raw, naked message of salvation. Every night, he took altar calls. There was one man that used to answer that altar call and he would pray and pray and would not get through. He would cry and cry. After the third day, this man cried without getting through with God. Gift Smith walked to him and said, "Can I help?" The man said, "You cannot help me;" because I have been working in a company for nineteen years and there was no single day I didn't steal something home. Now you are talking about restitution and salvation. How can I restitute what I have been stealing every day for nineteen years? This is why I have been praying here every night and there is no breakthrough." Gift Smith said, "Okay, why can't you go to the owner of that company and tell him the truth." The man said, "If I go there, I will go to jail forever and I might die in jail. Then Gift Smith replied, "It is better for you to die in that jail and make heaven than for you to remain alive, perish and go to hell." Immediately the man heard that, he jumped up and ran straight to the owner of the company. When he got there, the owner of the company was smoking a heavy cigarette. The man said sir, "I came to confess my sin. I started here as a messenger and I became a manager. Every day, I stole something home. I want to surrender my life to Jesus. I have confessed my sin to him." The man said, "Okay, you know you are going to jail?" The man said "I am ready sir, if that is going to give me my peace." The owner of the company looked up at the face of the man and said,

THE TRAGEDY OF STEALING

"Okay, on second thought, if your life has changed like this, then I will make you the director of the company." He almost fainted. He ran back to the crusade. Gift Smith was still there and it took Smith time to hear what he was saying. He was so excited. The enemy has been saying, "Don't talk, if you talk, that is it."

We have counseling cases. The man already had children outside. Now he came and married another lady and didn't tell her that he has children outside before that marriage. Later, the woman found out and problem started. He now said, "General Overseer, help me to beg her not to go."

7. Refrain from gossip or rumour. What you cannot confirm, wash it out of your spirit. It would be a disaster for somebody to go to hell for spreading false information that originated from you.

8. Know how to say, "No." whatever you know is not right, turn it down.

9. Let the Holy Spirit in you get into gear before your mouth begins to talk.

DR. D. K. OLUKOYA

TENANTS IN THE GROUND FLOOR

> *But the fearful and unbelieving and the abominable and murderers and whore mongers and sorcerers, and idolaters and all liars shall have their part in the lake which burneth with fire and brimstone, which is the second death.* Revelation 21:8

What this implies is that liars are there at the bottom of hell fire. They would be the ones down below. They have even been rated more dangerous than witches and wizards.

Confess to God from your heart any falsehood in your life. You cannot build up anything that would last on a lie. You cannot build prosperity on lies. You cannot build what is not good and expect good to reign upon it. Even our fore fathers who didn't even read the Bible said that if you are building your house with saliva, just a little bit of wind would destroy it because the foundation thereof is bad. Are you telling lies to your husband, teachers or cheating in class, telling one party one thing and the other another thing? You grieve the Holy Spirit by living in sin and pretending before all. Confess any falsehood in your life to God.

PRAYER POINTS

1. Every damage that lies have done to my life, blood of Jesus wipe them away, in the name of Jesus.
2. O Lord, my God, help me in my helpless situation, in the name of Jesus.
3. My Father, my Father, my Father, restore me to Your heavenly agenda, in the name of Jesus.
4. Every stronghold of lie in my life be destroyed by fire in the name of Jesus.
5. Spirit of truth overshadow my life, in the name of Jesus.
6. Powers of my fathers house assign to make me miss heaven release me and die, in the name of Jesus.
7. O Lord my God release the grace to speak the truth always upon my life, in the name of Jesus.
8. Arrows of lie fired into my life go back to your sender, in the name of Jesus.

CHAPTER 5

THE Tragedy of Lies

THE TRAGEDY OF STEALING

The word of God is specially inspired to reprove, correct and instruct us all in righteousness. It provides an opportunity for us to examine our faith and amend our ways. Do you desire to live your life pleasing the Father always and in all things? Always read and apply the invaluable admonition in God's word to your life; you will become perfect and thoroughly equipped for every good work.

> *Ye worship you know not what we worship for salvation of the Jews. But the hour cometh, and now is, when the true worshippers shall worship the Father in spirit and in truth for the Father seeketh such to worship. God is a spirit and they that worship him must worship in spirit and in truth.* John 4:22

> *Ye are of your father the devil and the lust of your father ye will do. He was a murderer from the beginning and abode not in the truth Because there is no truth in him when he speaketh a lie he speaeketh Of his own for he is a liar and the Father of it."* John 8:44

The father of every liar is the devil. If we are telling lies, we are doing the devil's work for him. This is a serious problem in Christianity. It is not in vain that God wrote that they that worship Him must do so in spirit and in truth. Those are the kind of people God is looking for. We cannot over-emphasize the need for everyone to discard lying and cling to the truth. A lifestyle of truth and honesty is a hallmark of God's sons while that of lying is a trait of satan's children.

DISTINCTIVE CHARACTERISTICS OF TRUTH

Truth is a powerful entity. How far down the wrong road you have gone never makes it a right road. That you were born into a way and that you have travel that way all your life never makes it right. The calibre of human beings travelling a wrong road does not make the road right. Time never changes the truth. Truth is truth and it cannot be decided by majority vote. How many associates you have on the wrong road does not make the wrong road right. Truth will either bless you or shake you. Truth is immutable; truth is eternal. You will lose every battle you fight against the truth. Truth is very stubborn; it can never die. Those who spoke the truth died, but truth itself can never die.

The first scientists said that the world is flat because that time what we believe is that you can walk from one end to the other end straight, but the man say

THE TRAGEDY OF STEALING

the thing is like a circle. I think they killed that scientist; whereas if they had bothered to read the Bible, they would have read that God said the world is circle. Although they killed the man, truth did not die. That is why wherever truth is present, God is there. No matter whether the person speaking the truth is a believer or an unbeliever, God is there. But when you are lying, lying is always afraid of examination. The truth likes examination. Whatever happens, beloved, the truth must prevail. You may run for years with your lies, truth will catch up in one day.

There was this beautiful girl who came to church, but she was a serious hypocrite. She had a brother in the church who she promised to marry. She also had a boy friend she was dating in the school. So she was double-dating and lying to each brother. The mobile phone we now use has increased the number of people going to hell fire. Somebody sits beside another man's wife and tells his own wife that he is inside his office. That is how people are going about lying with mobile phone All liars are abomination to the Lord. The devil is their father. There is no small lie.

So, this sister wrote two letters: one letter to the brother in the church and another letter to the one in the school. But when she wanted to post the letters, she made a mistake. She posted the one she was supposed to post to the brother in the church to the brother in the school and the one for the brother in the school, she posted to the one in the church. That was how all the lies she had been telling crashed and blew into the open.

Take note of this fact: anything you know that you will be highly embarrassed to read to the congregation that you did, don't do it. Jesus said, *"What a man is saying inside his room or doing, on the last day, the person that would be proclaiming it would be at roof top."* All those things you have been hiding from people, everybody would know. They would know that you masturbate, fornicate, commit adultery and steal.

Everybody would know that you are deceiving your wife. Everybody would know that you are a liar. It would be a broadcast. The time to stop it is now. Judgment meets you the way death meets you. When we gather where somebody died, we say, "May their soul live in peace." It is a lie. Once the person didn't live well, the person will not rest in peace. The Bible says, *"It is given unto man to die only once after that judgment."* So, immediately you shut your eyes in death, you either land in hell fire or in paradise. There is no middle camp. There is no purgatory anywhere.

Truth is tough; it will not break, no matter what you say. If you are against the truth, then you have the whole universe working against you. And whoever you are, no matter how big you are, anytime truth is blocking your way, then you are heading towards the wrong direction. You better do a reverse. No matter what you believe, it doesn't change the truth. If you crush the truth in the head, it would rise again. If you ignore the truth, it would not kill the truth.

Truth Builds; Lie Destroys

Truth is always the strongest argument and truth never dies. Our ancient fathers told us that no matter how fast lies travel, the truth will catch it up. If you have members of your family in government, you better appeal to them not to go with lies. Enjoin them to stay with the truth because you can't fight the truth. It's a lion that will fight for itself. Truth is truth, even if everyone is against it. Lie is lie, even if everyone is supporting it. That's why I always advise people to be ready at all cost to hold on to the truth. Prefer to lose your situations than to tell a lie.

We handled a case not too long ago. A man had children outside and got married to a new wife, without telling that new wife that he had already had children outside. The new wife now discovered and said she was not willing to go on with the marriage. It is better to tell the truth. Be willing to go into fire than to worship the image of Nebuchadnezzar. Run the risk of being poor instead of becoming rich because of lying. All wealth accumulated by falsehood or lies will certainly collapse; it will backfire on children, grand children and great grand children.

If a person can sit down and decide to cheat or to lie, the person is a rotten human being. If your tithe is ten thousand naira and you bring two thousand naira, you are a liar. The Scripture reveals what happened to those who lied in the Bible days.

CONSEQUENCES OF LYING

Without truth you cannot call yourself a worshiper of Jehovah. When truth begins to decay, it becomes a lie. A lie is a deliberate untrue statement with the intention to deceive. Your mouth is your destiny. If you are using that mouth to tell lies, it would backfire. Perhaps your own lie is white lie, as in the case of Ananias and Sapphira in Acts 5. An untrue statement that appears harmless and unimportant. There is what we call half truth. It is the kind of lie Abraham told.

There is deception. There are some people we call pathological liars. You can lie through commission; you can lie through omission.

THE TRAGEDY OF STEALING

I remember when we got here in 1994, we wanted to construct benches for the church and a lot of carpenters applied. It was as if there was going to be a fight. I now gave the job out to about seven of them. I shared the benches for them to do. When they finished constructing them, I now packaged their money and put excess. Only one of them came back and said, "Daddy, this money is more than what I did." That was how I eliminated all the others. Only that honest one was doing the work. And the others were complaining, "Why did you give everything to this man?"

When you lie, it hinders your own blessing. You can lie by carrying rumors promoted by gossip. You can lie by flattery. You can lie by slandering people. You can even lie by keeping quiet.

No man has a good memory to be a successful liar. One day you would forget that you have lied before. Lies must have cloths on. Truth is very naked. Lie is a cripple. A half truth is a whole lie. Then before you say you are deceiving others, the first person you have deceived is yourself. If you add or subtract to the truth, it makes you a liar. A lie can travel half-way round the world while the truth is just putting on its shoes, but it would catch it up. A lie may take care of the present but it has no future. What the Bible calls sin has many key holes, but it is a lie that fits on all the key holes of sin. That's why people who do a lot of kneeling in prayers don't lie. Most of those who lie are not prayer warriors.

Sometimes, how well you sleep depends on how little you lie. Exaggeration is the twin brother of falsehood. The truth may hurt you but lying is an agony. When a lie is deliberate it is a sinful heart. Don't run after lie; live it alone. There is a spirit of lying because it is easy to tell many lies, but difficult to tell only one truth. Human beings are born a truthful people but most of them die as lairs. When you are applying cream to change your colour, you are a liar. No liar ever prospers for a long time.

A lot of people tell lies when they feel that the truth is dangerous. Instead of telling somebody simple truth, you prefer to lie. It is a very strange matter that people would be copying the devil.

In Revelation 21:8, the Bible says, **"But the fearful and unbelieving and the abominable and murderers and whoremongers and sorcerers and idolater and all liars, shall have their part in the lake which burneth with fire and brimstone which is the second death."**

WHAT YOU SHOULD DO

You need to repent if you have been lying.
You need to decide to constantly tell the truth.
You need to depart from the life of falsehood.

THE TRAGEDY OF STEALING

What do you think important that you can achieve or do with a stolen identity? You should not lie because the Bible says the truth shall set you free. You should not lie because if you keep lying it becomes a habit that would be very difficult to break. Lies make satan your father, so you should not lie. Liars don't get away with their lies. People respect honest people, not liars. I agree that telling the truth may be tough. You can't please everyone. You need to stay in the arena of the truth.

Are you a truthful person? Are you lying before your children? Do those children know mummy and daddy as lairs? Are you a hypocrite before them? There are many parents in this church, their children are lost. They are not coming to church with their parents because of their attitude to the children at home. They refuse to bring Christ to their home.

PRAYER POINTS

1. My Father, deliver me from the lies I am telling myself, in the name of Jesus.

2. My Father, have mercy on me and deliver me to the uttermost, in the name of Jesus.

3. Powers exposing me to darkness, die, in the name of Jesus

4. Every poison in my body, I am not your candidate, die in the name of Jesus.

5. Power assigned to convert my life to a dustbin, die in the name of Jesus.

6. I pull down every stronghold of lies in my life and my family in Jesus name.

7. Powers assigned to disgrace me, your time is up, die.

8. Ancestral oracle speaking against my family, shut up in Jesus name.

9. Satanic dedication of my family, die in the name of Jesus.

▶ CHAPTER 6

Five-Fold Prescriptions *for* Overcoming *Stealing*

- Holiness: Key for Triumphing over Stealing
- Restitution
- Contentment
- Hardwork: Antidote to Poverty and Stealing
- Pray Stealing Out of Your Life

1. HOLINESS: KEY FOR TRIUMPHING OVER ALL SINS

God has an effective prescription for sin and its destructive influence. It is holiness within and without. A life of complete purity will keep God and his holy angels constantly with you, just as it will shield you from the attacks of the devil and his demons. Resolve to make holiness within and without your watchword and lifestyle today.

Holiness is total submission of your body, soul and spirit to the Lord. Every aspect of your life is under His control. Your talking, your dressing, your work and all you do are under His control. Holiness starts from within. Once it starts from within, then nobody needs to be preaching to you on what not to wear or do. You would know that this is not holy behaviour. The trouble these days is like the story they used to tell us in our primary school days.

There was a king who had a beautiful daughter. The king decided that he was going to give out his daughter to the fastest runner. Immediately that competition was announced, most of the animals there did not bother to contest because they knew that the dog would win. So the dog came and registered his name for the race. But to the amazement of everybody, the second day, the tortoise showed up to register as well. We all know the tortoise is a sluggish animal; it moves like a snail. When the tortoise registered, everybody laughed at him and said, "How can this tortoise compete with the dog in a race?" But the tortoise spent the day before the race to do his home work very well.

A day to the race, the tortoise went to the market, bought very juicy bones and planted them in strategic places on the race track. The day of the race came and the umpire said, get set, go. The dog took off and tortoise crawled after him. But as the dog was moving away, he perceived that there was a bone nearby. The dog left the race tracks, went to the bone and started eating it. As he was eating it, something reminded him that he was in a race, but he kept saying, Tortoise is a slow animal. "I will finish the bone and still win." The dog took off again, a few meters away another big bone was by the side. The dog could not resist the bone. He went there again and started eating that one. And do you know, while the dog was still eating juicy bones, the lazy sluggish tortoise won the race.

Satan has handed over bones to many Christians. They are busy licking it seriously. The three pillars of faith have been replaced with many things in many churches today. The word of God in many places has been replaced with motivation and entertainment words. Prayer has been replaced with singing, clapping and the performance of comedians. The Holy Spirit has been replaced too. Many church members don't speak in tongues; they did not receive the baptism of the Holy Spirit. They would say "Once my heart is clean…"

Note beloved, God does not manage people. God does not share people. It is an insult for God to be sharing you with malice, fornication, adultery. That's why God said if you are lukewarm, I will spit you out of my mouth. I want you to think deeply about this issue. God does not bother about majority. He has never been interested in a crowd. He wants quality not quantity.

Enoch preached, only eight people were saved. God was not bothered. Only Abraham was called out of that idolatrous land. God was not bothered. Gideon gathered about thirty two thousand soldiers, God needed only three hundred. Six hundred thousand men left Egypt, only two got to the Promised Land, God was not bothered. Jesus, after working for three and half years, preaching and teaching and healing, gathered only one hundred and twenty people in Jerusalem. God was not bothered. I want you to check your life. Holiness is essential; you need to connect to the holiness of God. Holiness is allowing God to perform His work of grace in your life. Check your life seriously, understands that without that holiness no man shall see the Lord.

Finally, God would always forgive every sinner who comes for forgiveness. He will not turn any one back. However, forgiveness of sin never removes the consequences of sin. This is why you need to be holy. Sin would sometimes leave a scar in your life that forgiveness cannot clear. To take God's forgiveness for granted is to risk uncertain consequences, and the results you may not even know. Forgiveness will wipe away a sin, but not the consequences of that sin, which most times, would be more painful than the sin itself. The Bible talks about the wages of sin. Sin is a bad pay master who has never paid anybody well. The commission on sin is usually worse than the profit it gives to you. The Bible says "though hand be joined in hand no sinner would go unpunished." So, if you form the habit of regularly committing sin and ask God to forgive you. He may forgive you, but you will certainly bear the consequences. God forgives and will ever forgive while grace lasts, but forgiveness never erases the scars of sin. The consequences of sin are always greater than the pleasure it had provided. The water of sin may be sweet, but the consequences would always be bitter. That's why the Bible says without holiness no man shall see the Lord.

HOLINESS AVERTS DANGER AND PRESERVES BELIEVERS

Jesus said, "The prince of this world cometh unto Me; he found nothing." If the prince of the world should come to you now, will he certainly find nothing in you? One satanic agent by name Emmanuel Eni, many years ago published a book called 'The Book of Deliverance from the Power of Satan.' He was into darkness, occult and dark spirit world before he surrendered to Jesus. In that book, he said he went to an all night prayer meeting and found people singing and dancing. He looked around and three quarters of them that are dancing and shouting, "Down down, Satan," if they decided to them, they would all be finished. It means they were living unclean lives. Do you still watch pornography? You can't connect to holiness and you remain an enemy of God. You still lie, steal, fornicate and you come to a praying church, you should be advised that you cannot connect to that holiness. Once you don't connect to holiness and

THE TRAGEDY OF STEALING

there is danger about to happen, God would not rescue you from that danger because when you were alive you were of no benefit. That is why, at times, if something dangerous is about to happen and a child of God is going to be involved, if he is precious in the eyes of the Lord, the Lord takes him out. If it is the one living unclean life, a double life, he would be wasted together with others.

A woman gave a testimony at our church in Abuja. She boarded a bus. When she had sat down, she remembered that she had not bought something. She jumped down to go and buy it. She came back into the bus, but someone had taken her seat. There was one seat left, so she sat down. Then she remembered that there was still something to buy again, she jumped down to go and buy it. When she was came back, the conductor said, "You cannot enter. You are not serious. This is the third time you are jumping all over the place." He called on another passenger to replace the sister and the sister waited for the next bus. Ten kilometers away, a trailer fell on that bus that left, everyone there was crushed. God took the sister away from that tragedy because she was living a life that God respects.

Beloved, note also that Jonah was in a boat because he decided to be unholy by disobeying God. God wanted to wipe out Jonah and whoever was travelling with him in that boat. So because of

Jonah everybody in that boat would have lost their lives. But there was another man of God, Paul. He was in the ship with two hundred and seventy two people. All those people were to be wasted, but because Paul was there, the Lord preserved all those people. Paul was living a life of holiness. He was not living in disobedience.

2.   RESTITUTION

The Bible enjoins every believer to follow peace with all men, have a clear conscience and good testimony. God introduced the doctrine of restitution to achieve these noble objectives. Restitution pre-dates the law and has been taught and practised throughout the dispensations. Moses, the kings and prophets as well as the church age (the time of Jesus Christ, the apostles up till now) all confirm the relevance and importance of restitution in man's relationship with his fellow men and in obedience to God.

Restitution is the act of restoring to the rightful owner something that has been taken away, lost or surrendered. It is the act of making good or compensating for loss, damage, or injury; indemnification. It is also a return to or restoration of a previous state or position.

THE TRAGEDY OF STEALING

What Does the Bible Say About Restitution?

God commands that we make restitution; His Word teaches and guides us on why, when and where restitution is necessary. More importantly, God's Word teaches us how to make restitution as well as the benefits inherent in making restitution. Some of the relevant scriptures on the subject of how to make restitution read:

> *A thief must certainly make restitution, but if he has nothing, he must be sold to pay for his theft. If the stolen animal is found alive in his possession whether ox or donkey or sheep, he must pay back double. If a man grazes his livestock in a field or vineyard and lets them stray and they graze in another man's filed, he must make restitution from the best of his own field or vineyard. If a fire breaks out and spreads into thorn bushes so that it burns shocks of grain or standing grain or the whole field, the one who started the fire must make restitution. If a man borrows an animal from his neighbour and it is injured or dies ... he must make restitution. Exodus 22:1, 3-6, 14.*

Leviticus 6:2-5 covers other situations in which the stolen property is restored, plus one fifth of the value. Also of note in this passage is the fact that the restitution was made to the owner of the property (not to the government or any other third party).

The Mosaic Law, then, protected victims of theft, extortion, fraud, and negligence by requiring the offending parties to make restitution. It also implies that making amends with one's neighbor is just as important as making peace with God. Restitution, both in the Old and New Testament, is God's way of ensuring social justice, peaceful co-existence and social engineering.

Therefore, we make restitution because God commands it (Lev. 6:1-5; Ex. 22:10-13). We make restitution because it enables us to have a clear conscience towards God and towards man (1 Sam. 12:1-5; Acts 24:16). Lastly, we make restitution because it proves that we are saved, broken and are willing to live in obedience (Luke 19:8-9; Ezek. 33:14-16).

When Do You Make Restitution?

i. At all times and as long as you live.
ii. As often as the Holy Spirit convicts you.

Benefits of Restitution

The benefits of restitution are as numerous and far-reaching as other commandments of the Lord that a believer obeys. Some of them are as follows:

To the Individual

- It enhances the person's fellowship with the Trinity.
- It makes him/her completely guiltless; hence victory over the "Accuser of brethren" (Rev. 12:10).
- It is a catalyst for revival both spiritually and physically.
- It enhances one's prayer life, giving one boldness and confidence to worship God and pray.
- It enables or facilitates holy and righteous living (Zachaeus repented, and his sincerity was evident in his immediate desire to make restitution. Here was a man who was penitent and contrite, and the proof of his conversion to Christ was his resolve to atone, as much as possible, for past sins).
- It helps to make heaven.
- It brings prosperity into all areas of the person's life.

In the Church (Body of Christ), it is a means of:

- Eradicating corruption.
- Exposing evil works and workers.
- Making members work together with the same mind.
- Being in unity and with singleness of heart.
- Faithful commitment and loyalty in the work of God.
- Church growth and development.

In the Community:

- It promotes business relationships i.e. people can do business together without any fear.
- It prevents oppression of the less privileged, poor widows in the society.
- It promotes justice and fairness.
- It promotes peace and tranquility.
- It prevents crime and criminal activities.
- It protects people from being cheated, short-changed or duped.
- It enhances protection and security of lives and properties.
- It also enhances interpersonal relationships and interactions.
- It prevents crises, clashes and wars.

THE TRAGEDY OF STEALING

Have you stolen, picked or converted someone else's property to your personal use? Return the thing to the person or organization that owns it. If you have been robbing God by not paying your tithe and giving your first fruit offering, you have to restitute and restore all you have unlawfully taken according to biblical standard on restitution.

Have you destroyed, damaged or vandalized something that belongs to another person or have you injured or maimed another person and had kept quiet all these while? You have to replace that thing or pay compensation for the injury as enjoined by Exodus 22-:5-6 and Exodus 21:18-19.

Remember that God is no respecter of persons. In the Bible, He instructed King Abimelech to make restitution and the king did. It was when the king obeyed God by restoring Sarah to Abraham and by adding a sheep, oxen, men servants, women servants and thousand pieces of silver as gifts that Abraham prayed for the king, his wife and maidservant and the LORD opened the wombs of the house of Abimelech which he had closed because of Sarah, Abraham's wife (Genesis 20:6-18). Abimelech obeyed and was blessed for it.

Another Bible character that made restitution was Zacheaus, during the earthly ministry of our Lord, Jesus Christ. He declared to Jesus and all around him that he was willing to amend his ways and live right by restoring four times whatever he had defrauded anyone of or stolen. Jesus said, "Today salvation has come to this house." Zacheaus' repentant spirit enabled him to make restitution and earned him salvation.

This shows the connection between repentance and restitution. Genuine repentance births restitution and restitution births divine pardon, salvation, approval and numerous other benefits. Although restitution may not be a condition for salvation, repentance is and God's grace imputed to us when we are saved leads us to closer and deeper walk with God and enables us to obey the law of restitution and be at peace with God and man.

3.   CONTENTMENT

God has called us, His children, to a life marked by contentment. He has also offered contentment as one of His five-fold prescriptions for overcoming greed and stealing. Contentment does not mean you will never want anything else. It means you can be satisfied when you are on your way to where you are going. A person that lacks contentment is never satisfied. He or she always wants more. Lack of contentment gives birth to murmuring and greed which in turn engender stealing.

A contented Christian has overcome the pervasive influence of materialism; he is not a captive to Mammon and is satisfied with what he has. He is living in compliance with the Bible's admonition that says:

> ***Let your conversation be without covetousness; and be content with such things as ye have: for he hath said, I will never leave thee nor forsake thee.** Hebrews 13:5*

Contentment is the attitude of accepting what God provides and being happy with it. Greed creates perverted values and drives people to crave for and steal what belongs to others. In 1 Timothy 6:6-8, Apostle Paul encouraged believers to make contentment a lifestyle and revealed the true source and meaning of contentment.

> ***But godliness with contentment is great gain. For we brought nothing into this world, and it is certain we can carry nothing out. And having food and raiment let us be content therewith.** 1 Timothy 6:6-8*

First, Apostle Paul reveals that contentment comes from making godliness, not gain, our focus and priority. By this, he means that those who preoccupy themselves with living to please God in all things and at all times rather than amassing wealth and material gains shall enjoy contentment. It is the inordinate and insatiable desire to have more of material things coupled with the failure to put premium on the supernatural or the misplacement of priority that makes discontent and steal.

Second, Apostle Paul shows that contentment comes from having the right understanding that the eternal outlasts and is more rewarding than the temporal. The eternal refers to seeking first the kingdom of God and His righteousness. Those who live for the temporal seek things of this world that are short-lived. He posits that those who live for the eternal, not the temporal experience three facets of contentment: freedom from greed, freedom from anxiety and freedom from circumstances as the basis for happiness.

As someone wrote, contentment does not seek for gratification in what is not needed, and does not seek happiness in the shallow things of life. Apostle Paul who wrote that godliness with contentment is great gain is an example of what he preaches. He

had learned the secret of contentment in every circumstance of life. (Philippians 4:11-12). According to Apostle Paul, we can have contentment by taking the following is six steps:
1. Give thanks in all things
2. Rest in God's providence
3. Be satisfied with little
4. Live above life's circumstances (2Cor. 12:9-10)
5. Rely on God's power and provision (Philippians 4:13)
6. Be preoccupied with the well-being of others (Philippians 2:3-4; Ephesians 3:24)
7. Give yourself, talent and possessions to God and His work.

4. HARDWORK

Hardwork is the antidote to laziness, poverty and stealing. When God created the Garden of Eden and put Adam in charge of it, He gave Adam work to do: he was to cultivate it. Again, when He pronounced the first blessing on man, He said: "Be fruitful and multiply, replenish the earth and subdue it." Replenishing and subduing the earth involves work. So God enjoins man to work; He does not condone laziness.

The Scripture also reveals that Jesus worked. He had an occupation which he practiced before His earthly ministry fully began:

> *Is not this the carpenter, the son of Mary, the brother of James, and Joses, and of Juda and Simon? And are not his sisters here with us? And they were offended at him.* Mark 6:3

Jesus Himself affirmed that the Father works when He said, **"My Father is working until now and I am working."**

Hardwork or labour is another prescription of the Most High for overcoming stealing. His Word through Apostle Paul confirms this:

> **Let him that stole steal no more: but rather let him labour, working with his hands the thing which is good, that he may have to give to him that needeth.** Ephesians 4:28

It is important to note the three prescriptions here:

➢ Stop stealing.

➢ Work and earn a living legitimately.

➢ Cultivate the habit of giving to those in need.

THE TRAGEDY OF STEALING

Giving is a cure for stealing. The Bible further buttressed this in one of Apostle Paul's writing:

> *I have shewed you all things, how that so laboring ye ought to support the weak, and to remember the words of the Lord Jesus, how he said, It is more blessed to give than to receive.* Acts 20:35

Apostle Paul was the best example of what he preached. He worked as a tentmaker to provide for himself and not bring God's name and work to ridicule. He encouraged us not to be lazy and idle, but to work and give to God and the needy from our income or profit. Again, the Lord condemned laziness and encouraged work in these words:

> *For even when we were with you, this we commanded you, that if any would not work, neither should he eat. For we hear that there are some which walk among you disorderly, working not at all but are busybodies. Now them that are such we command and exhort by our Lord Jesus Christ, that with quietness they work and eat their own bread.* 2 Thessalonians 3:10-12

The truth is that those who engage themselves in work and earn decent living do so in obedience to God and will not miss their reward. It is also such individuals that will obey the commandment, Thou shall not steal." There is dignity in labour and giving to God and His work, as a habit, can help conquer the spirit of stealing.

In the words of a writer, stealing takes from others with no thought of giving in return. Justice demands that when one takes, he must give one something equal in return. Christianity teaches us to give freely with no expectation of getting something in return. These writer's words are true. The Bible also prescribes giving as a cure for stealing.

5. PRAY STEALING OUT OF YOUR LIFE

Prayer is the most potent and most formidable power God has given man. Prayer changes things and you can use it to dislodge whatever you do not want out of your life or to bring what you desire into your life. Prayer makes the impossible possible, surmounts the insurmountable and reverses the irreversible. Through prayer great oppositions are subdued and obstacles are removed. It is the most reliable force for doing exploits in God kingdom. It is as important to the saint as oxygen is to man's existence. Those who avail themselves of its power and privilege get promoted to the class of the supernatural and take their rightful position in the affairs of heaven and man.

THE TRAGEDY OF STEALING

Prayer is the secret of champions in the Kingdom of God. We must always pray to prevail, excel and reign. Also, we should all pray that God fills us continuously with the spirit of grace and supplication.

Are you caged and manipulated by the spirit of stealing? You can have your deliverance through targeted, militant and aggressive prayer. Set time aside to inquire of the Lord about the root cause of the ungodly habit in your life. Confess every known sin to the Lord and repent from them. Do restitution where necessary and ask God to have mercy on you and help you. Then, take authority over the spirit of stealing, bind and cast it out of your life and command it never to return. Make quality decision to live a life of holiness, contentment, hardwork and giving. As you trust and obey God in all things, He will make all grace abound towards you, grant you sufficiency in all things and make you to abound in every good work.

PRAYER POINTS

1. Lord, make me what You want me to be, in the name of Jesus.
2. Dullness of heart, dullness of ears, disappear in my life, in the name of Jesus.

3. Every power, that has turned my life upside down, roast by fire, in the name of Jesus.

4. Oh Lord my God, re-arrange my destiny according to your plan, in the name of Jesus.

5. No evil vow, decision or prophecy shall come to pass in my life, in the name of Jesus.

6. My life, will not be used by the devil, in the name of Jesus.

7. Every hole in my hand, be sealed by the blood of Jesus.

8. Every evil door that I have used my hand to open for the enemy to come into my life, close by the blood of Jesus.

9. O Lord, let me touch heaven today and let heaven touch me, in the name of Jesus.

10. In the name of Jesus, spirit of stealing, you will not prosper in my life.

11. Holy Ghost Fire, burn away every satanic deposit in my life, in the name of Jesus.

12. Every satanic investment in my life, be wasted, in the name of Jesus.

13. Satanic agenda for my life, vanish, in the name of Jesus.

14. I refuse to give the accuser of the brethren any legal ground in my life, in the name of Jesus.

15. Every good thing stealing has destroyed in my life, be restored back, by fire, in the name of Jesus.